CALLED UP

Resources by Dave Dravecky

Dave Dravecky (Today's Heroes) (with Tim Stafford)
Do Not Lose Heart (with Jan Dravecky and Steve Halliday)
Glimpses of Heaven (with Jan Dravecky and Amanda Sorenson)

*Stories of Life and Faith from
the Great Game of Baseball*

CALLED UP

DAVE DRAVECKY
with Mike Yorkey

GRAND RAPIDS, MICHIGAN 49530 USA

ZONDERVAN™

Called Up
Copyright © 2004 by Dave Dravecky and Mike Yorkey Creative Services, Inc.

Requests for information should be addressed to:

Zondervan, *Grand Rapids, Michigan 49530*

Library of Congress Cataloging-in-Publication Data

Dravecky, Dave.
    Called up: stories of life and faith from the great game of baseball / by
Dave Dravecky with Mike Yorkey.—1st ed.
       p. cm.
    Includes index.
    ISBN 0-310-25230-X
    1. Christian life.   2. Baseball—Religious aspects—Christianity.
I. Yorkey, Mike.   II. Title.
BV4501.3 .D73 2003
242'.68—dc22   2003022952
                                                          CIP

This edition printed on acid-free paper.

The website addresses recommended throughout this book are offered as a
resource to you. These websites are not intended in any way to be or imply an
endorsement on the part of Zondervan, nor do we vouch for their content for the
life of this book.

Published in association with the literary agency of Alive Communications, Inc.,
7680 Goddard Street, Suite 200, Colorado Springs, CO 80920.

Interior design by Michelle Espinoza

Printed in the United States of America

04 05 06 07 08 09 /❖ DC/ 10 9 8 7 6 5 4 3 2 1

●●●

To Byron Ballard

Without your help,
I might not have been called up.

●●●

We want to hear from you. Please send your comments about this book to us in care of zreview@zondervan.com. Thank you.

GRAND RAPIDS, MICHIGAN 49530 USA

WWW.ZONDERVAN.COM

CONTENTS

INTRODUCTION

"The one constant through all the years,
Ray, has been baseball. America has rolled by like an
army of steamrollers. It's been erased like a
blackboard, rebuilt, and erased again. But baseball has
marked the time. This field, this game, is part of our
past, Ray. It reminds us of all that once was good, and
that could be again. Oh, people will come,
Ray. People will most definitely come."

—Terence Mann (played by James Earl Jones)
talking to Ray Kinsella (played by Kevin Costner)
from the 1989 film, *Field of Dreams*

During eight seasons of playing major league baseball, I learned
more than the importance of getting ahead in the count or wasting
a pitch when I had the batter in the hole with an 0–2 count. Baseball taught me a lot about life and about my relationship with God.
I learned incredible lessons about what it meant to be a Christian in
a worldly, money-soaked profession played before sellout crowds in
gleaming new stadiums and in the living rooms of America. I
learned that cheating by scuffing the baseball may earn a pitcher
baseball immortality, but that doesn't earn immortality with God. I
learned that teammates were watching my every move, so I had to
walk the talk. I learned that Satan had a sneaky move to first base,
but if I kept close to God's bag of truth, he wouldn't pick me off.

At the same time I was learning these timeless lessons, I had
the greatest time playing professional baseball. To become a major
league baseball player is to jump into the sandbox of life: you play
a game for a living, you get paid ridiculous amounts of money,
and everyone is your friend. I believe this great game is still the
national pastime, especially for families. There's nothing like

multi-generations—grandparents and parents and grandkids—watching a baseball game together. I don't care if the game is being played at Yankee Stadium or a Little League diamond in a neighborhood park. Pitches are thrown, batters take swings, and fielders make plays. Baseball has a wonderful rhythm that hasn't changed for nearly 150 years. Three strikes and you're out. Take your base on four balls. You have to touch first, second, and third base before you can come home. The game's not over until the final out. Baseball keeps you young. As Willie Mays once said, "You've got to have a lot of little boy in you to play this game."

This reminds me of what Jesus said in Matthew 18:3: "I tell you the truth, unless you change and become like little children, you will never enter the kingdom of heaven." That is, we should have the attitude of a trusting child when we approach God. I like having a childlike attitude of trust and faith when it comes to my relationship with Christ. It's kind of like someone saying, "You've got to have a lot of little boy (and little girl) in you to trust in the Lord."

That's just one of the few similarities I see between baseball and our Christian faith. We're drafted to play on his team (the Angels?), whether we deserve it or not. We have the fundamentals drilled into us—getting the lead runner, hitting the cut-off man, taking the extra base—just as we study the fundamentals of our faith in Sunday school and Bible studies. We step into the batter's box with the chance to make the most of our at bat, just as we hope to make the most of our interactions with others for Christ. Once we're running the bases, we're dependent on the third base coach, who can see the entire field of play while we're running for glory. We need to follow his direction so that we reach our heavenly home without getting thrown out.

In *Called Up,* I draw on my on-the-field experiences and retell classic baseball stories from today and yesteryear to illustrate how God doesn't waste any pitches when it comes to teaching us something about him and his Word. Mike Yorkey, who grew up watching Padre baseball in his hometown of San Diego (and witnessed the Padres' first game in 1969 as a teenager), has provided invaluable assistance in researching and writing this book with me. You're going to love the short stories, the quick applications, the timeless thoughts, and the funny and insightful quotations.

For instance, consider the wit and wisdom of Yogi Berra, the great New York Yankee catcher who once said, "You've got to be very careful if you don't know where you're going, because you might not get there." There's a lot of spiritual wisdom packed in that statement. If we don't know where we're going to spend eternity, then we won't get there. Jesus tells us that he is the way, the truth, and the life, and no one comes to the Father except through him. That's why we have to know where we're going.

That's just one small sample of what you'll find in *Called Up*. You're going to have a grand old time reading this book. Are you ready to get going? Good, because I think I just heard the umpire yell out, "Play ball!"

LEADING OFF

1

The one player I hated to see step into the batter's box was Tim Raines, a speedy shortstop who played much of his career with the Montreal Expos. Tim did not swing a home-run bat, but he was a line-drive hitter who could hit for average, beat out ground balls for base hits, and regularly turn singles into doubles when the outfielder didn't hustle to cut off the ball.

Tim was one of the best base-stealers of my era. If you walked him or held him to a single, he was a threat to steal second *and* third because of his blazing speed and uncanny timing. Everyone knew that his coaches gave him the green light when he roamed the base paths. Tim was such a base-stealing threat that my coaches continually harped on me to keep him close. "Give the catcher a chance to throw him out," they said.

Tim worked hard to get into the head of the pitcher once he took his lead. I know he tried to get into mine. My number-one priority was to get the hitter out, but when I took my stretch and watched Tim inch his way to a bigger and bigger lead, I was supremely aware that he was a huge threat to go at any time.

Tim knew that I knew that he knew he could steal second base just about any time he wanted to. He also knew that he had flustered hundreds of pitchers over the years to the point of distraction. Distracted pitchers "lose" the next batter by giving up a base on balls or delivering a fat pitch that results in a "gapper" all the way to the wall. Believe me, you give Tim Raines a running start, and he could score standing up on an extra-base hit.

That's why I concentrated very hard when Tim took his lead off first base. I focused on the job at hand: keep Tim close, stay ahead in the count, and make good pitches. Don't make a mistake. Keep your focus.

I've tried to keep that single-minded focus in my Christian life. Focusing on God's Word has become so important to me that I work hard not to be distracted. I do that through prayer, fellowship, and regularly reading God's Word. I'm not perfect in these areas, not by a long shot. But these are all things we can do on a consistent basis, which will help us not be distracted by the everyday happenings of life.

What do you do to remain focused in your Christian life? Are you reading your Bible each day? Attending church consistently every Sunday? Participating in a weekly Bible study, especially a men's group? Don't forget: Satan knows that you know that he knows he can distract you with the "busyness" of life. If the Great Deceiver can distract your spiritual attention away from God's Word and fellowship with other believers, he can run wild on your base paths.

Nope, you never want Satan even to reach first base. Punch him out with your best pitch—a single-minded desire to follow Jesus Christ.

Belonging to the Chatter Class

When the San Diego Padres called me up in 1982, I felt as if I was the greenest rookie ever to put on a big league uniform. For the first couple of weeks, I tiptoed around the clubhouse as if I didn't belong there. I kept my head down and my mouth shut.

Once the game started, however, I wanted to help out the team anyway I could, so I cheered from the bench. I guess I could still hear my old Little League coach bellowing, "Let's hear some chatter, guys."

So I chattered. I yelled at the opposing pitcher ("You're losing it, Two-Nine!") and jumped up whenever one of our guys made a great play or stroked a big hit. I was first in line to shake the hand and slap the back of our home-run hitters. In those days, the high-five, bashing forearms, or rapping knuckles hadn't been invented yet.

I guess my cheerleading bothered a few of my "cooler" teammates. One time, shortstop Garry Templeton—one of the flashier players in the game—eyed me after one of my leather-lunged outbursts.

"Dave, calm down," he ordered. "You're in the big leagues now."

I felt every teammate's eyes boring down on me.

"Sure, Tempy," I mumbled. "Anything you say."

Later that night, however, I began to have second thoughts. Wasn't I playing a kid's game? Wasn't it *funner* to play baseball that way? What's wrong with having a good time at the old ballpark?

I decided that I would have a "kid's game" attitude for as long as I was in the big leagues. Of course, I tempered my enthusiasm whenever Tempy was in the neighborhood, but by golly, I would keep up the chatter.

And I sure had fun doing it.

They Said It

"I bleed Dodger blue and when I die, I'm going to the big Dodger in the sky."

—Tommy Lasorda, Los Angeles Dodgers manager

"Wait until Tommy meets the Lord and finds out that he's wearing pinstripes."

—Gaylord Perry, Hall of Fame pitcher

A SAD SHOW

2

Baseball fans think that when major league ballplayers leave the game—or are handed their pink slips—that we traipse off to our winter retirement homes in Arizona, kick off the shoes, and watch ESPN *SportsCenter* around the clock.

Believe me, even listening to Chris Berman say "back-back-back-back" can get old. For most people, loafing around is okay for a few months, but most of us are eager to *do* something, whether it's opening a pizza parlor or starting up a Web site that sells gum chewed by Luis Gonzalez and Sammy Sosa.

Once the cheering stops and you have to reenter the "real world," it can be difficult to adapt, even if you have millions in the bank to comfort the blow. Some struggle more than others. Some of my former teammates didn't handle the post-baseball years very well. Alan Wiggins, a second baseman-turned-junkie, died of AIDS after being infected by a needle. Pitcher La Marr Hoyt was arrested at the Mexican border with a trunk full of drugs. John "The Count" Montefusco was arraigned before a judge for beating up his wife.

Then there's the sad tale of Eric Show[1] (rhymes with *pow*), who was a pretty good pitcher in his day, winning more games in a Padre uniform than anyone in franchise history. When I was called up to The Show for the first time in 1982, one of the first persons to greet me was Eric Show. As far as I was concerned, Eric was a borderline genius, who not only knew the Bible inside and out but could expound on philosophers such as Kant, Hegel, Freud, and Kierkegaard. He was an accomplished jazz musician who self-produced several albums. He liked to think big thoughts and study God's Word intensely. I was a

---

[1]Eric is an answer to a trivia question: Who was on the mound when Pete Rose stroked his 4,192nd hit to overtake Ty Cobb for most hits in a career?

new Christian at the time—and a lightweight when it came to heavy thinking—but this charismatic pitcher took me under his wing even though I had nothing to offer him.

When we were on the road with time to kill, Eric invited me and a fellow pitcher, Mark Thurmond, to study the Bible with him. Those were some intense sessions. Articulate and self-assured, he could preach without notes at our Sunday Baseball Chapels or share his testimony on cue before church and community groups. Eric was such a natural born leader that I never minded when he challenged me to live a deeper life for God. As I said, he was one studly Christian.

Yet for all his biblical knowledge and leadership acumen, Eric was a hurting individual. No one, not even I or my teammates, knew he was struggling with drugs. Eric couldn't let his guard down, lest anyone think he wasn't the person that everyone thought him to be.

No one knows when Eric started abusing heroin and cocaine, but he had a couple of bizarre episodes after he left the Padres. The Oakland A's cut him after he couldn't explain why he showed up to training camp with nasty cuts on both hands. At the age of thirty-four, Eric was out of baseball.

It was a huge shock to hear the tragic news on a March day in 1994: Eric Show was found dead in his bed, the victim of a massive heart attack after taking a "speedball"—a toxic mixture of heroin and cocaine. He was only thirty-seven years old. The newspapers made hay out of the story, taking great lengths to point out that Super Joe Christian was just another junkie. A total hypocrite. Someone who wasn't what he said he was.

Those things weren't true. I was devastated to hear of Eric's death because I was so close to him. We'll never know who the demons were that Eric couldn't get out. They kept the rally going by stepping up to the plate and feasting on what he was serving up. With each extra-base hit, Eric felt more and more alone, until he believed he was the only one left on the field battling those demons.

I'm sorry that Eric never asked for bullpen relief from his friends. I would have loved to do anything I could to be there for him. If he had only owned up to the gravity of the situation, I'm sure that someone in his life or myself would have tried to help him. I take away three lessons from Eric Show's sad story:

1. If you're hurting, don't be afraid to ask for help. Give others the opportunity to pick up for you.
2. Be available to those who hurt. Ask God to direct you to friends and to give you the right words to say.
3. Develop friendships with friends with whom you can openly share your heart. Eric didn't have those types of friendships, and it cost him his life.

Moonshot

In 1963, baseball pitcher and lousy hitter Gaylord Perry told the assembled media, "They'll put a man on the moon before I hit a home run."

On July 20, 1969, a few hours after Neil Armstrong set foot on the moon, Gaylord Perry hit his first, and only, home run.

God sure has a sense of humor.

They Said It

"They brought me up with the Brooklyn Dodgers, who at that time were in Brooklyn."

—Casey Stengel, when he was managing the
New York Mets in 1962

STEP ON A LINE, AND YOU'RE DOING FINE

3

The next time you go to a major league baseball game, watch the pitcher after the third out of the inning is made.

I predict two things will happen:

1. He'll walk slowly toward the dugout, head down and looking very much like a young college professor walking across campus, lost in thought.
2. When he reaches the baseline, he'll change the cadence of his walk to make sure that he doesn't step on the chalk line that runs from home plate to the outfield wall. In other words, he'll do everything but make a long jump to make sure he doesn't step on that line.

When that happens, the pitcher is following a time-honored superstition as old as the game itself. Lefty O'Doul, a Yankee pitcher back in the 1920s, summed up the prevailing mood for today's hurlers when he said, "It's not that if I stepped on the foul line I would really lose the game, but why take a chance?"

That wasn't my attitude. I *squashed* the baselines. I made sure I drove my foot into the chalk. I wanted no part of that superstition— or any others I saw practiced by my teammates. Besides, I never believed that striking out the first batter of the game meant I would win the game, just as I didn't believe that striking out the first batter meant I would *lose* the game. No four-leaf clovers in my back pocket for me.

Not all my teammates felt the same way. I remember one superstition: if you touched one young prospect, he had to touch you back. You should have seen the other players sneak up and poke him with a finger, and then hightail it to the trainer's room while he chased after them.

Baseball players are always looking for something to bring them good luck. Joe DiMaggio and Willie Mays always touched second base when they ran to the outfield or ran back to the dugout at the end of an inning. Perhaps they did it out of habit, since much of baseball involves routine. We drive the same route to the ballpark, put on our uniforms, play nine innings of baseball, and go home. All that routine partially explains why some players seek a superstitious groove to ward off any hexes or jinxes.

Wade Boggs, a great hitter in the 1980s and 1990s, always ate chicken before every game, and he set up a twelve-day rotating schedule of recipes he liked. Eating chicken sounds better than what the New York Yankees did one year when they were slumping. Lou Gehrig's mother sent a jar of pickled eels to the clubhouse, which got passed around. (Yuck!) When the Yankee batters sent ricochets into the alleys later that afternoon, the entire team bellied up to the pickled eel jar and made sure they ate some eels before the game.

I knew players who were very superstitious about what they wore. There were players who had to wear the same socks—or the same underwear!—night after night to keep a hitting streak going. In 1986, Charlie Kerfeld of the Houston Astros sported a George Jetson T-shirt under his uniform before every start. He finished 11–2 that year. Toronto Blue Jays catcher Rick Cerone donned long johns under his uniform while playing in frigid temperatures before one April game. Rick, not noted for his batting skills, got on an early season hitting streak. He figured it had to be the long johns, so he wore them *all* season long, even during the hot summer months. I'm not sure what Rick was thinking because he finished that year with a career-low batting average of .239.

On another occasion, Minnie Minoso of the Chicago White Sox went hitless at the plate. It had to be the evil spirits on his uniform, so after the final out, he walked straight through the locker room to the community showers, where—still dressed in full uniform, cleats included—he turned on the nozzle. The next day, he banged out three hits. After that game, eight teammates ran for the showers and let the water cascade on them with their uniforms still on.

On a more serious note, during my last full season in the big leagues in 1988, the Houston Astros lost eleven consecutive games. Pitcher Jim Deshaies purchased a book on witchcraft with the intent of warding off the evil spirits surrounding the club. He gathered twigs from four different trees, performed a spitting ritual, and then burned the twigs in the locker room as he invoked special chants. First baseman Glenn Davis, who was a Christian brother, was noticeably skeptical. The weird thing is that the Astros won the following night and Glenn pulled a hamstring muscle.

I would have been like Glenn—noticeably cool to warding off evil spirits. Ballplayers may slavishly perform superstitions in the belief that doing so will bring good luck that day, but after I became a Christian, I knew that God was bigger than luck. I could trust in him for the outcome, which freed my mind mentally. It sure was easier suiting up before a game without worrying whether today was my "lucky" day.

The Old Testament is full of warnings to stay away from fortune tellers and interpreting omens, but a verse from Proverbs puts a positive spin on the topic: "If you stop listening to instruction, my child, you have turned your back on knowledge" (19:27, NLT). I'm going to keep listening to God's instruction instead of the silly ways many use to curry favor with the baseball gods of good luck.

The Rite of Rituals

Having made my speech about superstitions, I'm all for rituals.

No, I'm not talking about religious rituals, those ceremonial things done by rote every Sunday at 10 A.M. I'm talking about those little habits or movements that baseball players do over and over before the pitcher goes into his windup. You've seen these rituals a million times, I'm sure. Before every pitch, the pitcher steps off the mound, rubs the ball with both hands, climbs back atop the mound, sweeps the rubber with his right foot, bends over at the waist, looks to the catcher for a sign, shakes his head no before nodding yes, and then rocks into his windup and fires away.

Meanwhile, the batter is going through his own set of rituals between pitches—tapping home plate with the end of his bat, rolling his shoulders, tapping the top of his helmet, taking several practice swings, and then waggling his bat while waiting for the delivery.

Rituals are different from superstitions. You do something in a superstitious manner because you think it'll give you good luck—or ward off the bad mojo. A ritual is something entirely different, something that gives the body a framework for what you have practiced. Nomar Garciaparra pulling on his batting gloves and tapping his toes between pitches is a ritual; Wade Boggs eating chicken before every game was a superstition.

Baseball rituals—going through the same pre-pitch routine, for instance—give you discipline and comfort. Rituals tamp down the butterflies and allow you to focus on the task at hand. Rituals give you a sense of control and stability in an unstable environment. They give you structure before every pitch and a way to cope with nervousness. I went through many of the time-honored pitching rituals that I just described, which gave me time to clear my mind before making my windup.

When it comes to having "rituals" in our spiritual lives, I realize that some church denominations place a greater emphasis on ceremony and rites. Again, there's nothing wrong with that, but things skitter out of control when preachers say that if you worship God in a prescribed order, he will look with favor on you—that if you follow the right rules, you can get to heaven.

That's a pitch way off the plate. Jesus said in Mark 7:7–8, "They worship me in vain; their teachings are but rules taught by men. You have let go of the commands of God and are holding on to the traditions of men."

True Christianity doesn't work that way since we can't "work" our way to heaven. Instead, my idea of a good ritual is starting off the day with some quiet time with God, reading his Word, and seeking direction from him.

Now that sounds to me like a ritual worth practicing. . . .

Don't Jinx Him

One of baseball's unwritten rules in the dugout is that you *never* talk to a pitcher when he has a no-hitter going. It's supposed to bring him bad luck if, between innings, you say something like, "Hey, Hightower, did you know that you're pitchin' a no-hitter?"

So when Shawn Estes, a New York Mets pitcher, had a no-no going in the fifth inning, everyone's eyebrows raised a notch when the JumboTron operator at Shea Stadium made sure everyone at the park was aware that indeed, Shawn Estes had not allowed a hit so far in the game. Estes lasted two more innings before his no-hitter was broken up in the seventh inning. Afterward, Mets manager Bobby Valentine was asked whether Estes had been "jinxed" by the JumboTron message.

Said Valentine: "I don't believe in superstitions. They're bad luck."

They Said It

"When a fielder gets the pitcher into trouble, the pitcher has to pitch himself out of the slump he isn't in."

—Casey Stengel, New York Yankee manager

THE UNDERGROUND TAPES

4

You might have not noticed it, but we recently celebrated the twenty-fifth anniversary of probably the most celebrated post-game interview in baseball history.

I'm not talking about Hank Aaron's interview after he broke Babe Ruth's all-time home-run record, or Reggie Jackson referring to himself as the "straw that stirs the drink" on the New York Yankees ball club. What I'm referring to is the profanity-laced outburst from Tommy Lasorda, the colorful Los Angeles Dodgers skipper who never met a plate of pasta that he didn't like—or resisted uttering certain four-letter and seven-letter words in his workday speech.

Tommy's profane blowup—with the offending words bleeped out—became an underground classic on the *Jim Healy Show* on L.A. radio for many years. It all started during a regular season game between the Los Angeles Dodgers and Chicago Cubs on May 14, 1978. Dave "King Kong" Kingman, a six-foot, six-inch-tall Cub outfielder known for either whiffing the air or launching rainbows into the left field stands, was a one-man wrecking crew against the Dodgers that afternoon. Kingman slugged three home runs, added a single, and knocked in eight runs, including a three-run shot in the fifteenth inning that proved to be the difference in a 10–7 Cub win.

After the final out, a handful of reporters gathered in the Dodger manager's office to fish for "quotes"—those nuggets of insight that writers drop into "game stories" for the newspaper. I can remember facing a battery of media types after nearly every game I pitched. We had an agreement: they would ask the same old questions ("How was your curveball working tonight, Dave?") if I could feed them something they could print ("I seemed to be having real good movement tonight, especially when I got Darryl Strawberry looking in the eighth").

Tommy knew he wasn't live that afternoon, so I'm sure he conducted himself accordingly. It started moments after the tough loss when Paul Olden, a stringer for Associated Press Radio, thrust a microphone in front of Tommy's jaw and asked a rather innocuous question: "What is your opinion of Kingman's performance?"

Maybe Tommy forgot to take his Metamucil that morning, but he was in a sour mood after losing that extra-inning game. Here's an edited transcript of that exchange:

Paul Olden: What's your opinion of Kingman's performance?
Tommy Lasorda: What's my opinion of Kingman's performance? What the @#$% do you think is my opinion of it? I think it was @#$%. Put that in. I don't @#$%. Opinion of his performance?!! @#$%, he beat us with three @#$% home runs! What the @#$% do you mean, "What is my opinion of his performance?" How could you ask me a question like that, "What is my opinion of his performance?" @#$%, he hit three home runs! @#$%. I'm @#$% off to lose that @#$% game. And you ask me my opinion of his performance? @#$%. That's a tough question to ask me, isn't it? "What is my opinion of his performance?"

I'm not going to be too judgmental on Tommy's choice of language since I've dropped a few f-bombs in my life. The point I want to make is this: words, once uttered, can never be retrieved. In fact, you can go to Dave Kingman's Web site, click on 1978, and hear the actual interview, with the profane words bleeped out.

I shudder when I read in Scripture that I will have to account for *every* word on that Day of Judgment. Matthew 12:36 warns, "And I tell you this, that you must give an account on judgment day of every idle word you speak" (NLT). The NIV version said we will have to account for every "careless word."

Yikes. That has me sweating more than a bases-loaded jam in the bottom of the ninth and we're up one run.

Swearing Off Swear Words, Part II

"When angry, count four; when very angry, swear," said author and humorist Mark Twain many years ago, but from what I've seen—and heard—very few ballplayers bother to count to four before spewing forth a torrent of profanity after the ump makes a bad call.

Four-letter words—including a particular twelve-letter one—were so much a part of the major league scene that they became like white noise to me. During my entire career, I heard a steady hum of swearing words sprinkled among speech. It was almost as if you were *expected* to swear so you could relate to teammates in the locker room or on the bench, much like a junior account manager is expected to use the words "branding" and "business model" when giving a presentation to upper management.

After I became a Christian during my first year of minor league ball, I couldn't help but notice the constant overuse of f-words and s-words in baseball. But something else surprised me: the constant taking of the Lord's name in vain. I didn't like it because saying "Jesus Christ" in an angry, swearing manner is insulting to the person who died on the cross for our sins. (Besides, why pick on the Creator of the Universe? Why not say, "Oh, Hitler!")

The Bible tells us that because of his obedience and sacrifice, "God highly exalted him, and bestowed on him the name which is above every name, so that at the name of Jesus every knee will bow, of those who are in heaven and on earth and under the earth, and that every tongue will confess that Jesus Christ is Lord, to the glory of God the Father" (Philippians 2:9–11 (NLT).

Instead, I heard ballplayers blow off Jesus Christ, and that bothered me. Unfortunately, I never confronted these guys on this, and I regret that. God's name should be holy and glorious, but these days, it's just another profane phrase. My teammates probably did not know that God takes the misuse of his name rather seriously. Exodus 20:7 says, "You shall not take the name of the LORD your God in vain, for the LORD will not leave him unpunished who takes his name in vain" (NLT).

When Hollywood made the movie *Hardball* a few years ago about a white Chicago father forming Little League teams in the inner city, the director felt it was necessary to have the African-American kids swear like sailors on shore leave, even though it was against league rules to swear. Bob Muzikowski, the real-life Little League coach on whom *Hardball* was loosely based, sued Paramount Pictures to bleep out the offending words, but he was thrown out at the plate by the judge, who ruled in favor of Hollywood's "artistic merits."

There's nothing artistic about going to the gutter and using street language. I can think of all sorts of reasons why swearing is bad for society. First of all, it's a lazy way to talk because if you listen closely, people deploy f-words and drop s-bombs instead of thinking of more descriptive adjectives. Besides dumbing down the culture, swearing is disrespectful to others and can escalate discussions into over-the-top arguments. Whenever you see a steaming-mad manager and an irate umpire going at it, you can be sure that they are exchanging more than neighborly pleasantries between them.

With all the swearing going on inside the lines, I noticed more and more fans incorporating their favorite blue words when they razzed the opposing team or yelled out after the home club erred. That hasn't made the old ball yard family friendly, in my opinion.

The sad thing is that swearing is a habit, but habits can be changed. All it takes is a little practice and some determination.

They Said It

"Age is a question of mind over matter—
if you don't mind, it doesn't matter."

—Satchel Paige, the ageless Cleveland Indians pitcher

YOU CAN'T FAKE IT 5

You've got mail.

We sure did when I was playing. Each day before a home game, the clubhouse manager delivered fan mail by the sackful to the players. Lesser-known teammates usually received a handful of letters, but mountains of cards, photos, and requests to sign something deluged superstars like Barry Bonds. To keep up with that amount of mail had to be overwhelming.

Many of my letters contained Dave Dravecky trading cards asking for my autograph. I figured that "signing," as we called it in the clubhouse, was part of my job description, so I made it a personal policy to sign every baseball card or snapshot sent my way. I always thought in the back of my mind that there was a young kid expecting an autograph from his baseball hero. I was happy to oblige, although at times, keeping up with my mail was a daunting task. Still, I could not ask someone to forge my signature.

I couldn't help but notice how some of the stars handled their fan mail, however. Many enlisted batboys or clubhouse gofers to scribble their name on thousands of baseballs, baseball cards, and assorted memorabilia. While I understood the rationale, I still thought there was something dishonest about having others sign your autograph. In fact, I actually became upset when I saw high school kids forging a superstar's scrawl on dozens of baseballs.

What I witnessed in major league clubhouses was nothing, however, compared to the outright thievery practiced by unscrupulous fly-by-nighters who manufacture and sell celebrity merchandise. A major ring based in San Diego was busted when the Padres' Tony Gwynn noticed that baseballs signed with his name were fakes—and the balls were being sold in the Padres gift shop! In a high-profile raid following a three-year investigation, dozens were arrested when federal authorities confiscated ten million dollars' worth of baseballs, posters, trading cards, and other collectibles. They even found a baseball signed by Mother Teresa, if you can believe that. At the time, an FBI special agent stated at least 50 percent of the one billion dollar sports and celebrity memorabilia industry is forged.

There is nothing more worthless than purchasing a Sammy Sosa baseball that someone else signed. A signature is a stamp of approval, a valid testament that that person held the baseball while he indelibly penned his name for eternity—or until the ink fades. We attach great value to an authentic signature, and we should because an authentic signature is the real deal.

That's why I've always striven to lead a life of authenticity, especially when I am with my family. My wife, Jan, and my two children see the real me—what I'm like behind closed doors. Do I act in the same authentic way when it's just my family and I, or am I blowing my top and demanding my own way just because the world can't see me?

That's a tough question—one we can all ponder. Are you acting one way with others—a courteous, attentive, and helpful Dr.

Jekyll—only to turn into a roaring Mr. Hyde with your loved ones just because something didn't go right?

The answer is to live a life of authenticity, not some counterfeit that's obvious to those who really know you. After all, isn't your family—the people who know the best—able to spot a fake in the window?

Return of the Hose

I'm a stirrups and sanitary hose kind of guy. This is why I have never liked the baseball pants that go all the way down the leg and practically touch the top of the leather cleats, à la Barry Bonds. Nor have I liked the relaxed-fit trousers and baggy jerseys that more and more players have adopted in recent years. That's why I cheered when Major League Baseball and the players' union agreed to a uniform makeover: no more loose-fitting jerseys and pants that made players look, well, sloppy.

I like seeing stirrups again. It's nice knowing that the Boston Red Sox really do wear red sox.

They Said It

"The doctors X-rayed my head and found nothing."

—Dizzy Dean, explaining how he felt after being hit on the head by a ball in the 1934 World Series

TWENTY-SEVEN OUTS

6

I was never perfect. Few pitchers ever are. The closest I came to a perfect game was when I retired the first sixteen Dodger batters before Billy Russell beat out an infield single in the sixth inning. But those who set down the order one-two-three for nine straight innings—facing the minimum twenty-seven batters—enter baseball lore.

Don Larsen pitched a perfect game in the 1956 World Series, and the next Yankee to match him was David Wells in 1998. (Here's another trivia answer for you: Larsen and Wells both graduated from Point Loma High School in San Diego.)

A pitcher trying to get the last three outs of a perfect game is one of the most tension-high times in sports. Let's listen to Vin Scully, the Dodgers announcer, describe Sandy Koufax's attempt, as it was transcribed in *The Third Fireside Book of Baseball*, edited by Charles Einstein:

> Three times in his sensational career has Sandy Koufax walked out to the mound to pitch a fateful ninth when he turned in a no-hitter. But tonight, September 9th, 1965, he made the toughest walk of his career, I'm sure, because through eight innings he has pitched a perfect game.

The Dodgers were playing the Chicago Cubs at Chavez Ravine before 29,139—and a million butterflies, said Vinnie. Few Dodger fans chose to leave the game after the seventh inning, which most Los Angelenos do to get a jump on the traffic. Sandy had a *perfecto* going. Koufax got ahead of the first batter, Chris Krug.

> One-and-two, the count to Chris Krug. Koufax, feet together, now to his windup, and the 1–2 pitch: ball, outside, ball two.

[The crowd boos.] A lot of people in the park now are starting to see the pitches with their hearts. The pitch was outside. Torborg tried to pull it in over the plate, but Vargo, an experienced umpire, wouldn't go for it. Two-and-two the count to Chris Krug. Sandy reading signs. Into his windup, 2–2 pitch: fast ball got him swinging! Sandy Koufax has struck out twelve. He is two outs away from a perfect game.

Sandy struck out Joey Almalfitano on three pitches, prompting the Cubs to send pinch hitter Harvey Kuenn to the plate. Kuenn, a veteran player in the last season of a brilliant fifteen-year career, led the American League in hitting with a .353 average in 1959. He would not be awed by the situation.

Koufax pitched a strike, then "overthrew" twice by trying to put a little bit extra into his pitches. Behind in the count 2–1, Koufax had to settle himself. He didn't want to fall behind 3–1.

You can't blame the man for pushing just a little bit now. Sandy backs off, mops his forehead, runs his left index finger along his forehead, dries it off his left pants-leg. All the while, Kuenn is waiting. Now Sandy looks in. Into his windup, and the 2–1 pitch to Kuenn: swung on and missed, strike two. It is 9:46 p.m. Two-and-two to Harvey Kuenn— one strike away. Sandy into his windup. Here's the pitch: swung on and missed, a perfect game!

You couldn't hear Vin Scully for a minute or two as he let the roar of the crowd speak for itself. I wish I could have heard Vin make the call because Sandy Koufax was my childhood idol.

As perfect and masterful as No. 32 was on that September evening, it's impossible to live a perfect life off the field. You can't face every temptation that Satan throws at you and not sin. Ever since Eve handed Adam a baseball-sized apple and offered him a bite, we have been living under a curse of sin.

Thankfully, I don't have to be perfect in my spiritual life, and neither do you. But just because we aren't perfect doesn't give us a license to sin. When Jesus died on the cross for our sins, he completed the most difficult perfect game ever attempted—dying for the sins of mankind. "It is finished," the Lord said just before he expired.

Yes, Jesus finished in perfection, which only makes sense since he *is* perfect.

A Dainty Morsel, Indeed

Something ugly happened to my idol, Sandy Koufax, in early 2003.

Perhaps you remember it. Without naming names, the *New York Post* reported that a "Hall of Fame baseball hero" had "cooperated with a best-selling biography only because the author promised to keep it secret that he is gay. The author kept her word, but big mouths at the publishing house can't keep from flapping."

Ah, I wonder who this "Hall of Fame baseball hero" could be? Was it Sandy Koufax, who just so happened to be the subject of Jane Leavy's acclaimed biography, *Sandy Koufax: A Lefty's Legacy*, which had been released a couple of months previously? (A fine book, I might add. I enjoyed it immensely.)

Even Ray Charles could see that one. An intensely private individual since his retirement in 1966, Sandy's response was to take himself out of the game. He announced that he was severing ties with the Los Angeles Dodgers in protest, meaning in practical terms that he would no longer attend spring training in Vero Beach, Florida, as he had for nearly fifty years, no longer visit Dodger Stadium for Old-Timer's Day, and no longer participate in any Dodger-related activities. He said that he would not return to the Dodger family until News Corp., the media conglomerate that owns the *New York Post* and the Los Angeles Dodgers, sold the L.A. club. That was supposed to happen after the 2003 season, so I hope Sandy is back in the Dodger fold.

What a mess, and I'm hacked that some gutless writer in New York, hiding behind the cloak of anonymity, could print such garbage in an unattributed gossip column. The Book of Proverbs is dead-on about the subject of gossip, as King Solomon addressed the topic a half-dozen times. One of them says, "The words of a gossip are like choice morsels; they go down to a man's inmost parts" (Proverbs 18:8). Another take on this verse expresses it even better: "What dainty morsels rumors are—but they sink deep into one's heart" (NLT).

This gossipy item about Sandy's private life—and I don't believe it to be true—underscores the biblical truth that people eat up gossip just like they eat a tray of "dainty morsels" served at a party. Few people think that such slurs hurt innocent people, but they do. It's a shame that the shoe couldn't be on the other foot some time, and these writers could experience firsthand the biting incisors of hurtful gossip.

I'm glad that Sandy took his ball and went home. He deserved a lot better.

They Said It

"Ain't no man can avoid being born average, but there ain't no man got to be common."

—Satchel Paige, ageless pitcher

HE'S YOUR BEST FRIEND

7

I might not have been the smartest pitcher to take the hill, but I did learn something inside the lines, and it was this: Make friends with the umpire.

You never wanted to do anything to antagonize an ump and get on the bad side of his navy blue chest protector. When I played, you didn't challenge plate umps like Paul Runge, Doug Harvey, Joe West, or Bruce Froehming on a balls-and-strikes call. They could bury you if you so much as shot a sideways glance in their direction.

Pitchers who questioned calls soon found themselves facing an arbiter who could "squeeze" the strike zone into a shape equal to the dimensions of a Mercedes hood ornament. William Tell had a bigger strike zone when he shot an arrow at the apple sitting on his son's head. That's why I went to great lengths to never show up an umpire or antagonize him in any way. I wanted to win a friend because I wanted to give the ump every chance to call a crucial strike in my favor later in the game.

Another thing I learned was that every ump brought a different strike zone to the plate—a strike zone that could expand or contract during a game. In the early innings, most umps gave me a wide strike zone. I could pitch a ball two or three inches on the outside part of the plate and still get the fist pump and the strike call. But in the later innings, their strike zones tightened up. I guess the umps figured that you had to get the hitters out with your best stuff.

One of the few umps with a tight strike zone all nine innings, however, was Joe West. I could pitch a ball a good half-foot off the plate in the early going and still get a strike call from some umps, but not with Joe. Even if I zipped a fastball on the "black" (the rubber borders of home plate), odds were that I still wouldn't get the call.

Did I ever get upset with Joe? No way! This is what I wanted Joe to think: *You know, this kid isn't giving me a hard time. He's respecting my strike zone. I like that in a pitcher.*

One time on a "deuces are wild" pitch—2–2 count, two out, two men on with Joe crouching behind my catcher—I threw a backdoor slider that was probably an inch or two off the plate. The catcher didn't move his glove, and Joe bellowed, "Stee-rike three!" That punch out was crucial since the game was on the line, but I got the call because I had respected Joe's strike zone.

That's why I tell kids that if an umpire calls a ball, don't get upset. I remind them that since umps come in all sizes, they will see the strike zone a bit differently. I wish every ump had the same strike zone, but that's human nature.

That's why I'm grateful that God never changes. His strike zone—his rules for what's out of bounds and what isn't—is always the same, which is comforting. There have been times in my life when I've been outside God's strike zone, and I wish I hadn't been. I had no excuses because I knew what God's standard was.

What's been cool about God has been his response to those wayward times. Regardless of whether I met his standard, he continued to love me unconditionally and let it be known that his grace and forgiveness were always available to me. That unchanging, ever-constant characteristic of God never changes from the first pitch to the final out.

"Jesus Christ is the same yesterday and today and forever," says Hebrews 13:8, and if you ask me, we can take that standard and be confident that it will hold during every inning of life.

Out of the Strike Zone

I'm glad that I pitched in the National League, where umpires reputedly called low pitches as strikes. For years, however, umps in both leagues could not agree on what constitutes a strike. National League umps liked the low strike; American League umps called more strikes on high pitches. The varying strike zone is why players grumbled after interleague or World Series games about a certain ump's "interpretation" of the strike zone.

I'm not sure what there is to interpret. The Rule Book says that a batter's strike zone is the space over home plate that's between a batter's armpits and the top of his knees when he assumes a normal stance. If only this were true. You don't see the high strike—or the low strike—called consistently these days. But just as the strike zone has shrunk over the years, it has also widened beyond the seventeen-inch-wide home plate. A pitcher can throw the ball one or two inches wide of the black—the black lining around home plate—and still hear the ump cry out, "Steeee-rike!" All you have to do is watch a ballgame on TV and watch the overhead camera shots.

There was a big hullabaloo a couple of years ago when Major League Baseball decided to erase the distinctions and directed the umpires to start calling balls and strikes the same in each league. Nearly everyone connected with the game agrees that the umps' strike zones are still as inconsistent as ever. I mention this because pitchers *and* hitters need a strike zone that is the same yesterday, today, and tomorrow—otherwise, chaos will prevail and the majestic game will become a burlesque.

An example of strike-zone chaos occurred a half-century ago on August 19, 1951. Bill Veeck, the St. Louis Browns owner who wrote a book called *Veeck as in Wreck,* took a wrecker's ball to the game when he inserted three-foot, seven-inch Eddie Gaedel into the game as a pinch hitter. Actually, Eddie—wearing a uniform with 1/8 on his back—was a "pinch walker," thanks to his miniscule strike zone. The midget waved a menacing bat, although legend has it that Veeck told him that there was a gunman in the stands who would shoot him if he swung. Detroit Tigers left-hander Bob Cain busted up laughing as the tiny batter came to the plate. Between guffaws, Cain threw four straight pitches "upstairs" to Gaedel, who hunched over to shrink his strike zone even more.

Veeck's stunt, of course, was just that—a stunt—although word got out that Veeck planned to insert Eddie as a pinch hitter the next time the Browns really needed a run—like with the bases loaded, since he was sure to draw a walk. American League president Will Harridge put the kibosh on that idea, banning midgets from major league ball. That was little Eddie's first and last major league at bat, as the lords of baseball decided that pinch-hitting midgets turned the game into a travesty. No one would want to watch a major league game involving "vertically challenged" batters with miniscule strike zones, so it was a wise decision to put an end to such gimmicks.

The much greater threat to the integrity of the game, however, is the changing strike zone of arbitrary umpires. Batters and pitchers both feel cheated when an inept—or biased—umpire keeps changing the strike zone. Since baseball is a sport steeped in tradition and history, its cherished records link today's game with its rich heritage. But what if hitters could shatter long-standing records because they only have to worry about a strike zone that is less than half of what it was a generation earlier? Does that not cheapen the records they would supposedly break? The only way to maintain the integrity of the game is to adhere faithfully to the book, *The Official Rules of Baseball*.

In the eternal scope of things, the integrity of baseball is not very important, but the effects of no reliable standard of truth and no moral absolutes are devastating and long-lasting. The great news is that God does not change the standards. He is ever faithful and ever reliable, never missing a call. We can be confident that what constitutes a strike in God's strike zone yesterday still works today and will still be the same tomorrow.

Why Didn't I Think of That?

I have another Bill Veeck story that is more outrageous than sending midget pinch hitters to the plate. It seems that Bill once owned a minor league team in Milwaukee, and he constructed a fence that could be raised at will. It didn't take long for a visiting manager to notice that the outfield fence got taller when his team was at bat and lower when his team was in the field.

I guess Bill wasn't into absolute standards when it came to ballpark fences.

They Said It

"And Kansas City is at Chicago tonight, or is that Chicago at Kansas City? Well, no matter, Kansas City leads in the eighth, 4–4."

—Jerry Coleman, San Diego Padre radio announcer

LIKE FATHER, LIKE SON   8

I have coached my son, Jonathan, through Little League ball and up, and I can see why many coaches say that baseball not only builds character but it also *reveals* character. I say that because what makes the following story interesting is that Jonathan is so much like his father—me.

When Jonathan was in high school, I volunteered my time with my son's team at Colorado Springs Christian School. Bob Knepper, who pitched with me on the Giants, was the head coach at one time, and he had established the following principle: we are here to build character in the lives of these kids. Sure, winning is important, but it's not the only thing. We should try to turn every mistake into a learning opportunity for the kids.

One of those great "learning opportunities" involved Jonathan. Jonathan's team was up 8–2 in the top of the seventh and final inning. The visiting team had put their rally caps on and quickly scored three runs. The score was now 8–5 with nobody out.

I called time, strolled out to the mound, and asked for the ball. Then I waved Jonathan over from first base to pitch. Jonathan has pitched a great deal growing up, so I knew he could nail down a save for our team. For a young right-hander, Jonathan throws well. He has good control, sneaky speed, and a hard-breaking curveball. His windup is mirror image of mine since he is a right-hander and I was a southpaw.

In this particular game, Jonathan had inherited a mess. Runners were dancing off first and second, and he went into his windup. A line drive into the gap brought in two runs. A fly ball was caught, but a triple scored another run, and suddenly, Jonathan had a tie ballgame on his hands with a man on third.

The visiting team and their parents and fans were delirious, celebrating a six-run rally to tie the game. The plate umpire called time to make an announcement.

"We have reached the two-hour-and-fifteen-minute time limit," he bellowed. "We will play until we have a winner this inning."

Like many high schools, our league played under a time limit and a ten-run "mercy rule." What the umpire was saying is that we would finish the inning and then call it game—win, lose, tie, or draw.

Jonathan, however, who was upset at blowing a three-run lead, thought we were playing under "sudden death" rules. In other words, he thought the first team to break the tie won. He went into his stretch and looked at the man on third. Then Jonathan reared back and put something extra on the pitch—no doubt going for the strikeout.

Jonathan fired a heater into the dirt, which squirted under the catcher's glove to the backstop. My son ran to home plate to cover while the boy on third base sprinted home. The catcher retrieved the ball, but instead of flipping it to Jonathan so he could apply the tag, the catcher decided to hold the ball and beat the runner to home plate.

A cloud of dirt rose in the air. "Safe!" the umpire bellowed.

Jonathan thought the game was over. In a typical Dravecky response, he threw his hat and glove to the ground and began stomping on them.

"You're outa here!" yells the ump.

A look of shock came over Jonathan's face. He couldn't understand why he had been thrown out of the game, until we explained to him that the game wasn't over. We still had our at bats in the bottom of that inning. Colorado Springs Christian School went on to lose 12–9 that afternoon.

Later that night, we had a chance to talk about what happened on the ball field. I wasn't mad at him, but I gently explained how his temper had caused him to get chased by the umpire when the outcome of the game was still in doubt.

That afternoon turned out to be a valuable lesson for Jonathan as well as for me. "You know, I can't be angry with you," I told Jonathan. "I probably would have thrown my mitt, too."

A grin came across Jonathan's face. I knew he would be all right, and so was I.

A Game Played in Hell

One day the devil called St. Peter and challenged him to a baseball game. "Let's see who's better—my team or your team," said the devil.

St. Peter thought for a moment, then looked in his book to see who could be in his starting lineup. "Sure," he said, "let's play a game. But you're gonna lose because I have all the Hall of Famers here."

"Maybe so," replied the devil, "but I've got all the umpires."

They Said It

*"Today is Father's Day, so to everyone out there—
Happy birthday!"*

—Ralph Kiner, New York Mets announcer

WHAT SCOUTS CAN'T MEASURE   9

When you think of a scout in baseball lore, you picture a grizzled old guy with a battered and faded ball cap who's hung around a few too many batting cages in his day. He beats the bushes in the far-flung hinterlands, searching for the next Sammy Sosa or Vladimir Guerrero. He's a shrewd judge of talent always on the lookout for the parent club.

My father was a "bird dog" scout who worked informally for the Pittsburgh Pirates organization. If a young player in our community (I grew up in Boardman, Ohio) was tearing up American Legion pitching or mowing them down in high school ball, Dad would check him out. If Dad thought the young player merited a closer look, he would call the Pirates' front office, and they would send out a scout to evaluate the phenom in person.

Dad always said that the hardest thing for scouts to measure is a kid's heart. Sure, scouts can bring their clipboards and a practiced eye to the ball field, but they cannot put a Jugs speed gun on a young ballplayer's determination or desire to play. Scouts can time how fast a batter sprints to first base, but no stopwatch ever displays a player's passion to play baseball. What scouts do, said Dad, is patiently wait for tough situations to develop during a game: a pitcher going into his stretch with two men on, one out, and their best hitter digging in, or a shortstop trying to throw out a speedy runner from deep in the hole with the game on the line. How a player performs in those pressure moments reveals a great deal about his heart and his ability to rise to the occasion.

This is where we find ourselves frequently with our Christian lives. Think about it: we can "measure" our friends and acquaintances by the things that they do and say, but ultimately, it is what they do in crunch time that counts. They can talk a good game or even be pillars of the church, but if they don't have the right heart for God, they will get rocked when the game of life hits them hard.

From my perspective, I want God to look at me and say that I am a man after his own heart—something God said about David. Ever since David reared back and made the best pitch in the Old Testament Hot Stove League—by flinging a baseball-sized rock sixty feet, six inches right between Goliath's eyes (what I call a *real* knock-down throw)— he showed that he was a young boy after God's own heart. Yes, David pitched some mistakes later in life (for instance, he never should have let Bathsheba step into the batter's box), but his heart never changed toward God.

If a scout were noting how you "perform" as a Christian, what would he tally on his score sheet? What could he tell the Creator about your heart? Is it large for God, or does it beat weakly for him?

Place Your Order Here

I'm sure glad I didn't pitch a century before my major league career. Up until 1887, batters could request that pitchers throw a high pitch or a low pitch. I can just see myself pitching against Ken

Griffey Jr. and hearing him say, "C'mon, Four-Three, groove me a low one so I can golf it out of here."

I would have stepped off the mound and taken two steps toward the plate before yelling, "Don't be digging too deep a hole, Junior, because this pitch is coming for your ear!"

They Said It

"I'll tackle that bridge when I get to it."

—Charlie Manuel, Cleveland Indians manager

BASEBALL'S SCUFFLAWS   10

I'll never forget the time a well-known pitcher—you'd know him if I revealed his name to you—stood on the mound at San Diego's Jack Murphy Stadium back in the days when I was playing with the Padres.

One of our players tipped a foul ball into the netting behind home plate, and our batboy retrieved the ball—something he does a couple of dozen times a game. The batboy tossed the ball toward the bench, where one of our players picked it up and studied it like Yorick's skull in Shakespeare's *Hamlet*.

"Hey, Dave, get a load of this ball," he said, as he lightly tossed it to me.

I rotated the ball and quickly found the rather large scuff mark—a gash, really—across the mud-stained leather covering.

"Hey, this ball is scuffed," I remarked. When the pitcher scuffs a ball, it behaves differently. Pitchers throwing roughed-up balls can throw sinkers that drop a foot just as the ball reaches home plate. It's as if the ball dropped off the edge of a table. Plainly put, hitters can't touch a doctored baseball.

"How many balls do you think that jerk has scuffed today?" my teammate asked.

"Beats me," I said.

"I say we find out," said my teammate, who fetched a plastic five-gallon bucket out of the clubhouse.

Three innings later, we had filled the five-gallon bucket with official National League baseballs, all scuffed by one of baseball's premier pitchers.

"Look at this, Skip," I said to Padre manager Dick Williams. "We have someone defacing the baseball."

Williams grabbed a couple of baseballs, and at the beginning of the next inning, showed them to the plate umpire.

"My hands are tied," said the ump. "Unless I catch him in the act, I can't do anything."

"How many scuffed up balls do we have to show you?" asked Williams, who was starting to get confrontational with the ump.

"Listen, the league won't back me up on this, so I'm not putting my job on the line for you, Williams."

Everyone encounters situations like that. Pitchers get away with scuffing baseballs with a sharpened belt buckle, a hidden piece of sandpaper, even a thumbtack in the glove. Some of baseball's most famous pitchers have relied on cheating—that's what I call it—to win games and establish reputations that led to million-dollar contracts. Knowing that there were pitchers out there cheating was the most disturbing thing I experienced in Major League Baseball and left me with a sour taste in my mouth. The fans and the media elevate those people to an incredible level because of their success, but only those behind the scenes knew that these pitchers gained their success by their ability to doctor a baseball.

I never cheated when I stood on the mound. Sure, it would have been nice to scuff up a ball with my belt buckle or drown the ball in spit when I needed a big out, but cheating—from my perspective—was not part of my game. My feeling was this: *If I can't get you with the stuff I got, then I don't belong here.*

Frank Tanana, a contemporary of mine, admitted to doctoring baseballs when he pitched for the Texas Rangers. When he became a born-again Christian, however, he *knew* he couldn't scruff up a ball just because he needed an out. "Christ, the Lord of my life, doesn't allow it anymore," he said.

I admire what Frank did, but let me tell you something: it bothered me to pitch against scofflaws on the mound. What soothed my feelings then and continues to soothe my feelings today is that God is in control and he knows everything. "A good man is guided by his honesty; the evil man is destroyed by his dishonesty," Proverbs tells us (11:3, TLB). Yes, there will be a Great Accounting one day, when we will stand before the one who has recorded our every act, thought, word, deed—and pitch.

And you know who's going to win that matchup.

Busted Red-Handed

Joe Niekro and I wrapped up our pitching careers at about the same time. My last season was 1989, Joe's was 1988. The difference is that Joe broke in with the Chicago Cubs in 1967, the same year I was a fifth-grader.

Joe was a crafty pitcher, a knuckleballer who played mainly with the Houston Astros. He won 221 games, enjoyed two twenty-game-win seasons, and won a World Series game in 1987 while pitching for the Minnesota Twins.

But it was an incident earlier that season that Joe is most remembered for. Joe was pitching against the California Angels, and like my afternoon in San Diego, Angels manager Gene Mauch began noticing something wasn't right in River City. The baseballs coming out of the game weren't roughed up, said the Angels manager, they were "downright mutilated."

As if he was reading Mauch's mind, home plate umpire Tim Tschida threw up both arms and stopped play after three pitches had been thrown in the bottom of the fourth inning. Tschida and the other base umps surrounded Niekro and ordered him to empty his pockets.

Joe reached back into his pockets and pulled them out while quickly raising both arms above his head. Replays show that Joe let something fly out of his right hand—a casual move that resembled what a kid would do when he's caught red-handed with something he shouldn't have in his hand. *Oops! What was that?* The umps looked around and found a nail board that had fluttered to the ground.

Then the umps frisked the forty-two-year-old pitcher, and lo and behold, what do we have here? *Well, there's a small piece of sandpaper in his back pocket. Now how did that get there?*

Tschida gathered up the evidence, plus a half-dozen scuffed baseballs, dumped everything into a plastic bag, and dispatched the evidence to American League president Bobby Brown. Within a few days, Brown issued his decision: Niekro was suspended for ten games for using a "foreign object" to illegally deface the ball. The ten-game suspension amounted to a $43,000 fine.

In his defense, Joe said that he always carried an emery board and a small piece of sandpaper with him out to the mound. As a knuckleball pitcher, he explained, his nails had to be just so. Sometimes he filed his nails between innings, he said. But what about the sandpaper? He sweated a lot, so the sandpaper was a backup to the nail file.

Oh . . . kay.

These days, Joe's son, Lance, is a top prospect for the San Francisco Giants. Lance was eight years old when Dad got busted in

1987, and when he was asked about it, Lance said he had never discussed the incident with his father. He never asked him if it was true, nor did Joe raise the topic. One thing he has noticed about his father, though, is that he always has a nail file in his back pocket. "So maybe the truth is he actually did his fingernails with it," Lance offered.

Okay, even if we give Joe the benefit of the doubt, the fact that Joe never discussed what happened that day with his son speaks volumes to me. That certainly sounds as if he had something to hide. But let's agree for a moment with Joe's contention, which is that he kept an emery board and a piece of sandpaper in his uniform back pocket because he sometimes gave himself a manicure between innings. If that were true, then he should have kept the nail file and sandpaper in the dugout or given the objects to the trainer for safekeeping. Having them in his back pocket while he pitched gives an indication that he wanted to scuff up the ball.

First Thessalonians 5:22 says we should "avoid every kind of evil." Walking to the mound with a nail file on your person would be like walking into an adult bookstore with money in your pocket. That's not what you want to do! Sooner or later, you will get into trouble because you're in the wrong place. "Avoiding every kind of evil" means not putting yourself into situations where you can sin. If your friends ask you to watch a certain movie or peek at something on the Internet that you know would not be pleasing to God, then don't do it.

I can't definitely state whether Joe Niekro used that nail file for its intended purpose—to file his nails between innings. One thing I do know: God knows the truth, and that's good enough for me.

Shattering More than a Bat

I know I've been talking about pitchers doctoring the baseball, but I would be remiss if I didn't say something about Sammy Sosa's use of a corked bat during the 2003 season.

Sammy, in case you were marooned on a desert isle without ESPN pumped in by satellite, swung at a low and outside pitch—

let me tell you, pitchers love that—and grounded harmlessly to second base in a game against the Tampa Bay Devil Rays. Unfortunately for Sammy, he struck the ball at the tip of his bat, which caused his lumber to shatter into two large pieces.

It turns out that Sammy's bat wasn't all lumber. Someone had drilled a hole at the thick end of the bat, filled it with cork, and painted it black to match the rest of the big stick. The cork was there to see as plain as day, and the umps immediately tossed the Cub outfielder out of the game.

In many ways, Sammy's persona of a lovable slugger shattered like the bat he was using on that June afternoon at Wrigley Field, which is a crying shame because Sammy has done so much for baseball. Here is a major leaguer who plays the game with the wide-eyed enthusiasm of a Little Leaguer, who hops on two feet as he watches his monstrous blasts leave the friendly confines, and who acknowledges cheering fans with a two-fingered tap to his heart in a salute. With the way Sammy plays the game, you can tell that he hasn't forgotten that he grew up dirt poor in the Dominican Republic selling oranges and shining shoes.

Sammy said he inadvertently picked up a corked bat that he used during batting practice. Players debate the effectiveness of corking their bats, but there are those who claim that the ball travels further when it "trampolines" off a corked bat. Sammy loves putting on a show at Wrigley, knocking batting practice pitches onto Waveland Avenue, so if a corked bat helped him get a buzz from the bleachers, then he would show 'em.

Major League Baseball confiscated nearly eighty bats from Sammy Sosa and X-rayed every one. Those bats were all clean; they were 100 percent wood, which was a good thing. But Sammy's reputation took a hit that fateful afternoon, which confirms the point I made with Joe Niekro: you have to be vigilant in maintaining your reputation. For grabbing what he says was a batting practice bat, Sammy's home-run prowess was questioned in the minds of some baseball fans.

Following the incident, I appreciated his willingness to admit that he made a mistake. That showed a lot of character. Sammy wasted no time publicly apologizing and acknowledging that he would accept whatever punishment the National League front office handed down. He owned up to his mistake, and baseball fans have by and large forgiven him.

Sammy knows he was lucky. The timeless words of King Solomon got it right: "A good name is more desirable than great riches; to be esteemed is better than silver or gold" (Proverbs 22:1).

Or a golden bat that hits home runs.

They Said It

"No, I didn't throw a spitter or a greaseball. And if I did, I wouldn't say it."

—Don Drysdale, Los Angeles Dodgers pitcher

"If you ain't cheating, you ain't trying."

—Chili Davis, outfielder during the 1980s and 1990s

WHAT'S IN A NAME?

I love nicknames, and if you hung around the Dravecky household for any length of time, you'd hear all sorts of nicknames bantered about. I answer to "Davey D," while I call my wife Jan "Janie Cakes." Meanwhile, my terms of endearment for my two children, Tiffany and Jonathan, are "Stinky" and "The Judster," respectively. I still call Tiffany—a.k.a. T. Marie—"Stinky" because I still haven't forgotten changing her diapers when she was an infant. As for J.D., my son Jonathan, he's always been "The Judster" to me. Fits him like an old T-shirt.

When I was pitching, my teammates gave me two nicknames—"Neck" and "Snacks." I think I heard some irate fans suggest several other nicknames, but my hearing's not too good. Besides, they must have been screaming them at me when I was being lifted for another pitcher and sent to the showers.

At any rate, my Padre teammate Mark Thurmond started calling me "Neck" shortly after I was called up because some cub reporter spelled my last name wrong, referring to me as Dave *Dranecky.*

Ha ha. Then when I played on the Giants, Kevin Mitchell noticed that I was always first in line for the post-game meal—"The Spread," as we called it. I loved eating after the game, and my enthusiasm for eating must have showed. Kevin called me "Snacks."

"Hey, Snacks, you make sure you don't take all the chicken," he would yell out from the back of the buffet line.

"I'll be sure to save a wing for you, Boogie Bear," I would yell back.

Nicknames are fun. You feel closer to someone when you know their special nickname. I remember playing with super-intense Will "The Thrill" Clark, our first baseman on the Giants. I loved walking past him in the dugout, late in a close game, and saying, "Thrill me, Will."

Good nicknames must do several things: capture a certain aspect of the person's personality, be endearing at some level, and sound good to the ear. A great nickname can catch the public's imagination and become a person's new moniker. Over the last century, the following players became known by their nicknames: Wee Willie Keeler, Babe Ruth, Cy Young, Shoeless Joe Jackson, Three Fingers Brown, Yogi Berra, Stan the Man Musial, Whitey Ford, Bo Jackson, and Goose Gossage, to name a few.

Sometimes nicknames become a player's persona. "Mr. October" pretty much sums up Reggie Jackson's career, as does "The Ryan Express"—Nolan Ryan. One of my pitching contemporaries in the 1980s had an All-Star nickname: Dennis "Oil Can" Boyd. This moody, flamboyant, and high-strung pitcher for the Boston Red Sox, who was plagued by a hot temper and persistent shoulder problems, received his unusual nickname from draining beer cans in his hometown of Meridian, Mississippi, where beer is called oil.

Today, everyone knows who the "Big Unit" is—towering Randy Johnson. "The Rocket" certainly fits Roger Clemens's blazing arm, and "Junior" is none other than Ken Griffey Jr. But every time I turn on ESPN *SportsCenter,* Chris Berman is cracking me up with another one of his clever and very punny baseball nicknames.

Chris started coming up with these wild nicknames when he was a history major at Brown University in the late 1970s. Many of them played off the Baby Boomer culture of sixties TV shows and rock 'n' roll bands. We first started hearing them in 1980 when Chris joined a new twenty-four-hour cable channel devoted to sports called ESPN as a *SportsCenter* host. As the highlight reel clicked, Chris tossed out his irreverent but all-in-good-fun nicknames. Besides, he could afford to take a few chances. The only people watching ESPN in those early years were his parents and some insomniacs in Fargo, North Dakota.

Legend says that Chris's first nickname was John Mayberry "RFD," followed by Frank Tanana "Daiquiri." Chris, who nicknamed himself "The Swami," says that he has two rules when coming up with his nicknames: they can't be derogatory and they have to be fun.

He's come up with more than a thousand of these charmers, and here are some of my all-time favorites:

- Rick "See You Later" Aguilera
- Roberto "Remember the" Alomar
- Bill Almon "Joy"
- George "Taco" Bell
- Barry "U.S." Bonds
- Scott "Supercalifragilisticexpiala" Brosius
- Tommy "Ben" Herr
- Tim "Purple" Raines
- Ruben "High" Sierra
- Kelly "Churchill" Downs

You won't find a thousand nicknames in the Bible, but you'll find your fair share. Jabez, the star of the phenomenal book *The Prayer of Jabez* by Bruce Wilkinson, is the Hebrew word for "pain." Apparently, Jabez's childbirth knocked down his mother like a high inside pitch because, as she says in 1 Chronicles 4:9, "I gave birth to him in pain." Unmollified by bringing a son into the world, she decided to name her son Jabez—or "Pain."

How would you like to go around life with such a weird name? *Now pitching for the Canaan Little Leaguers, Pain Jabez!* I'm sure the bench jockeys of his day rode Jabez unmercifully.

Names were a big deal in Bible times. Jacob, the twin son of Isaac, was given a name that meant "Grabber," which turned out to be fitting: Jacob grabbed the heel of his twin brother, Esau at birth, and later made a huge inheritance grab when he tricked his father into giving him his brother's birthright and "blessing."

Did you know that Naomi's sons, Mahlon and Chilion, meant "puny" and "pining"? No wonder they died before reaching manhood. In the New Testament, Simon was a plain fisherman who heeded Jesus' call to "Come, follow me" (Mark 1:17). Jesus chose him to be one of the apostles, and when he did, he gave him a classic nickname—a wordplay based on the Greek word *petros,* which means "rock": "And I tell you that you are Peter [a stone], and on this rock I will build my church, and gates of Hades will not overcome it" (Matthew 16:18).

I wonder what we're going to call Jesus in heaven?

Batter Up

Speaking of "The Spread," when you're on the road, the clubhouse manager for the opposing team is in charge of deciding the culinary lineup after the game. In St. Louis, we were usually fed something Italian—Chicken Cacciatore, seafood pasta, and deep-dish pizza. Montreal was another story. They usually put out a single chicken, and if you weren't at the top of the order, you were staring at a bony carcass during your pass-through. Nor was Los Angeles my kind of town. They served Dodger Dogs, which I always thought were leftovers from the concession stands.

I sure wish I was playing today in San Francisco, where the Giants have gone as much upscale as the players' salaries. Under the guise of providing more nutritious fare than Snickers bars, corn dogs, cheeseburgers, and fried fish, the Giants (and their trans-Bay rivals, the Oakland A's) are serving such diverse fare as sushi, halibut, turkey burgers, crawfish, and alligator. With so many millions invested in the players, management wants them powered by low-fat, high-protein foods, not junk food, so they've asked local restaurants such as MoMo's, Jardiniere, Tarantino's, P. F. Chang's, and the Hayward Fishery to cater "The Spread."

Yet, as many a clubhouse manager has learned, you can lead a man to tofu, but you can't make him bite. Maybe I would pass on the sushi and other raw fish delectables, but I could see myself chowing down on baked halibut or a delicious turkey burger.

All this makes me think: I wonder what "The Spread" will be like in heaven? I've got to think that every mouthwatering food will be set out on a buffet the length of a right field foul line, but the best news is that I won't gain a pound!

They Said It

*"A hot dog at the ballpark is better than
steak at the Ritz."*

Humphrey Bogart, Hollywood actor and baseball fan

GO WARM UP, SEAMHEAD   12

You can't surf the Internet very fast when you're pecking a keyboard with one hand, but I can get around the bases. Maybe I shouldn't be surprised by the treasure trove of baseball information available on gazillions of free Web pages, but I am. What does astonish me more, however, is the number of techies into baseball statistics.

Take Sean Forman, a computer nerd of All-Star proportions whose fingerprints are all over several Web sites, including Baseball

Primer (www.baseballprimer.com), Big Bad Baseball (www.bigbad-baseball.com), and Baseball-Reference (www.baseball-reference.com), a site that has compiled stats for every player and every game in major league history. You can find all sorts of interesting stuff, like:

- a list of players born on any single day
- standings from every date in major league history since 1901
- a script comparing any two players' teams or leagues
- a database of every major, minor, and independent league ballpark in the country

Forman, in his early thirties and an assistant professor of applied mathematics and computer science at St. Joseph's University, must be a bright guy. He is among a growing breed of those devoted to saber-metrics—the study of baseball statistics. Sabermetrics is derived from SABR, the Society for Baseball Research, which was established in 1971 in Cooperstown, New York, home of the Baseball Hall of Fame.

Forman and his fellow researchers really sink their teeth into baseball's most arcane statistical moments. I now present Exhibit 1 in which sabermetric researcher Chris Dial discusses some recent work that he and other researchers have done regarding some aspect of baseball. See if you can understand what he is talking about:

> Nelson Lu has a slot for "league average" and a slot for "replacement level" in the lists. We all understand, but "replacement level" is a more nebulous, ethereal mark. Nelson Lu defines replacement level, for his lists as 30 points of OBP and 30 points of SLG for RC/25 or 50/50 in RC/27. The reason is that in-season reports are RC/25 and only use regular players, while the end-of-season reports are RC/27 and include all players.

No, this isn't the talk of baseball statisticians with too much time on their hands. These seamheads love the game and analyzing base-ball's historical data; they just speak a different language than us, that's all. One thing we can all agree on is that baseball is probably the only game in which numbers are discussed, dissected, debated, and treasured *ad nauseam*. Batters are remembered for their batting average, number of hits, doubles, triples, home runs, base on balls, intentional walks, and runs batted in. Pitchers are judged objectively by their win-loss records, earned run averages, strikeouts, walks, and innings pitched, to name a few measurements.

I've always liked cold, hard statistics. No one could tell you how many touchdown passes Joe Montana threw in his career, but everyone knows that Babe Ruth hit 714 homers before Hank Aaron passed him. Barry Bonds immortalized the number 73 when he set the all-time season record in 2001. Even casual fans are aware that Joe DiMaggio hit safely in 56 consecutive games, Roger Maris smacked 61 homers in 1961, and Ty Cobb stole 96 bases in a single season. Even Alex Rodriguez's $252 million dollar contract figure has entered into numerical lore.

Another unique feature of baseball-reference.com is a listing of what Forman calls "Similarity Scores." Forman says stats guru Bill James introduced similarity scores in the mid–1980s with methodology detailed from his book *The Politics of Glory*. To compare one player to another, you start at 1,000 points and then you subtract points based on the statistical differences of each player. For pitchers, you would make the following deductions:

- one point for each difference of one win
- one point for each difference of two losses
- one point for each difference of twenty starts
- one point for each difference of twenty complete games

There are probably another ten more "differentials" that I will not list here. Who statistically compares to Barry Bonds? As you would expect, Barry ranks in the pantheon of all-time greats: Mickey Mantle, Frank Robinson, Ted Williams, Jimmie Foxx, Mel Ott, Mike Schmidt, Reggie Jackson, Willie Mays, and Harmon Killebrew.

I could not resist looking up whom I stacked up with statistically speaking. I wanted to know who my contemporaries were when you look across more than a hundred years of baseball. Who were the pitchers who put up similar career stats as me? Well, I found out on baseball-reference.com, and they were a list of nobodies: Wally Bunker, Jim Turner, High Bedient, Joe Broehling, Dave Rozema, Bernie Boland, Jack Kralick, Jimmy Lavender, Ferdie Schupp, and Bert Gallia. That'll keep you humble.

Another feature I loved on baseball-reference.com is called the "Oracle of Baseball," or a chain between two players. Let's say you want to know the link between Babe Ruth and Barry Bonds. You type their names into the appropriate boxes, click your mouse, and in less than a second, you receive this information:

- Babe Ruth (1914–35) played with Waite Hoyt for the 1922 New York Yankees.
- Waite Hoyt (1918–38) played with Bert Haas (1937–51) for the 1937 Brooklyn Dodgers.
- Bert Haas (1937–51) played with Minnie Minoso (1949–80) for the 1951 Chicago White Sox.
- Minnie Minoso played with Jim Morrison (1977–88) for the 1980 Chicago White Sox.
- Jim Morrison played with Barry Bonds for the 1987 Pittsburgh Pirates.

Isn't that amazing? There are just four players—actually, teammates who shook hands—that stand between the Sultan of Swat and the Giant slugger who may someday pass the Babe on the all-time career homer list.

But here's where I finally beat Barry in something. When I typed in my name to list the "Oracle of Baseball" from Babe Ruth to me, it took only three names!

Here is the oracle between me and Babe Ruth, who started out as a pitcher for the Boston Red Sox:

- Babe Ruth (1914–35) played with Dixie Walker (1931–49) for the 1933 New York Yankees.
- Dixie Walker played with Cal McLish (1944–64) for the 1944 Brooklyn Dodgers.
- Cal McLish played with Rick Wise (1964–82) for the 1964 Philadelphia Phillies.
- Rick Wise played with Dave Dravecky (1982–89) for the 1982 San Diego Padres.

You know what this "Oracle of Baseball" stuff reminds me of? All those "begats" in the first chapter of Matthew, in which the ancestors of Jesus Christ are listed in chronological order to prove that Jesus is the descendant of both Abraham and King David, just as the Old Testament predicted. The genealogy, in seventeen verses, refers to forty-six people spanning nearly two thousand years. That has to be the most impressive "oracle" of all time because it directly links Christ with Abraham, the founder of the Jewish nation, and David, the greatest king of Israel.

So the next time you skip over all those "begats," remember the oracle that started with Abraham, who played with Isaac, who played with Jacob, who played with Judah, and so forth, can be traced down the genealogical line to Christ's birth. That beats any oracle to Babe Ruth in my book!

Wanted: Someone to Sponsor Me

There's another thing I want to say about baseball-reference.com. The site, as I mentioned, is free, but there is no free lunch in this world. The Web site is a labor of love for Sean Forman, who spends hundreds of hours maintaining the site and adding more features each year. He figures that his "hard costs"—operating the server—are more than seven thousand dollars annually, so Sean came up with a unique way to seek donations.

Those who support the site with a ten-dollar donation, for instance, can "sponsor" any of a wide variety of pages on baseball-reference.com.

For instance, Ron Wood is the sponsor of the Willie Mays pages, which contain all his batting statistics over twenty-two seasons, fielding stats, and postseason play. When you sponsor a player, you're welcome to make a statement. Here's what Ron Wood said about Willie Mays:

> Mays could do it all, and did with a special elan. Willie starred in the first game I ever attended as a boy, and I was forever hooked on baseball.

Wasn't that nice? Now, here's your chance because the Dave Dravecky page has no sponsor! If you decide to become mine, can you let me know? I'd love to thank you in a tangible way.

Baseball Calculus

Moe Berg, a catcher for the Boston Red Sox in the 1930s and 1940s, offered to teach baseball to Albert Einstein in exchange for some math tutoring. Replied Einstein: "I'm sure you'd learn mathematics faster than I'd learn baseball."

The world's smartest man was on to something. Baseball is a game of permutations, precise throws, flare hits, and tape-measure home runs. It's a game of inches and split-second timing. And it's a whole lot more difficult to pick up than quantum mechanics.

They Said It

"Best player ever? I'd have to go with the immoral Babe Ruth."

—Johnny Logan, Milwaukee Braves shortstop

WE'RE ALL WINNERS

13

I think one of the most frustrating games I ever watched on TV was the 2002 Major League All-Star game. Perhaps you remember the one I'm talking about. After eleven innings of play, baseball commissioner Bud Selig called it a tie game after both managers ran out of pitchers, leaving fans with an unsatisfying 7–7 decision. Hey, if I had known they were looking for arms, I would have shown up at Miller Park in Milwaukee and given it a shot.

The attitude surrounding All-Star games has changed since I played in my only All-Star game in 1983. What an honor! Here was a kid from Boardman, Ohio, who was amazed just to be pitching in the big leagues, being picked to represent the National League All-Stars at the 50th anniversary game at Comiskey Park in Chicago. I had started the 1983 season with a 12–5 record, which earned me a spot on the team.

Manager Whitey Herzog gave me the ball for two innings—the fifth and sixth frames. I pitched against an American Leaguer team made up of heroes to me—Jim Rice, Freddie Lynn, George Brett, Cal Ripken (the Iron Man's first All-Star game, by the way), and the straw that stirred the drink—Reggie Jackson. I gave up no runs, punched out Fred Lynn and George Brett, and gave up just one hit to Jim Rice, who stroked a single between the third baseman and shortstop. What I remember is that I threw Jim the first change up I ever pitched from a major league mound. All I can say is that I'm glad the ball stayed in the ballpark.

My warm memories of that moment are a residue of the excitement I felt going up against the best baseball players on the planet. I really believed it was important for me to go out there and do my best and help the National League win. I cared about the outcome, and I know my fellow All-Stars cared who won or lost. We believed the National League had a reputation to uphold, but we got shellacked that day, 13–3.

I'm not so sure today's players see the interleague rivalry in the same light. Perhaps it's because players switch leagues and teams and allegiances so frequently because of free agency. I'll tell you what, though: the fact that I pitched two innings shows you how much the All-Star game has changed in the last twenty years. We did things different in our time. We pitched more than one inning. We batted more than once a game. Most of our frontline starters played more than two innings. We tried to win the game.

These days, managers treat the All-Star classic like a Little League game, making sure that no one gets his nose bent out of shape from not playing. The goal now is to play everyone on the thirty-man roster. That's what happened at Miller Park, as managers Joe Torre and Bob Brenly substituted freely, holding back one pitcher in reserve into the ninth inning. When the game remained tied and moved into the tenth inning, however, Torre and Brenly inserted their last pitchers—Freddy Garcia for the American League and Vincente Padilla for the National League. Each pitcher performed well; neither allowed a run in the tenth or eleventh innings. Since their managers didn't want to risk their arms a third inning, however, Bud Selig didn't have much of a choice but to call it a non-contest. In a sense, the All-Star managers painted themselves into a pitcherless corner by using nineteen pitchers in nine innings when they should have held two or three pitchers in reserve.

When the decision was announced that the tie game was over, angry fans pelted the playing field with garbage and rained boos and catcalls on the commissioner's box. They felt abused because they had paid $175 a ticket for this non-game. I could feel their pain. I, too, was annoyed that the game was not played to completion. Fans need some sort of closure when they invest three hours of watching a baseball game. They say that a tie game is like kissing your sister, and I can see why after viewing that debacle from Milwaukee. Everyone wants to see a winner and a loser, regardless of whether the game is a highfalutin All-Star exhibition or the seventh game of a World Series.

Contrast this to the direction taken by the Massachusetts Youth Soccer Association, which prohibits teams from keeping score in tournaments for players under twelve years of age. I guess the idea is to spare the kids the agony of defeat, but it also robs them of the thrill of victory. In this non-results-oriented environment, everyone gets a trophy since teams were banned from giving out trophies unless every player on every team got one.

I wouldn't be surprised if some of the people behind the anti-scoring movement are among those who don't think God is keeping score. We are told in Scripture that "God looks down from heaven on the sons of men to see if there are any who understand, any who seek God" (Psalm 53:2). That sure sounds like a Big Scorekeeper in the sky to me.

You know, I'm looking forward to getting my trophy when I go to heaven. I'm looking forward to the Lord saying, "Well done, my good and faithful servant," and giving me a pat on the rear end.

That's the All-Star team I want to play on.

They Said It

"Larry Moffett is 6–3, 190. Last year he was 6–6."

—Jerry Coleman, San Diego Padre radio announcer

THE GODS OF THE GAME

14

There's another All-Star team I would like to see play, but it's a team that I can see only in my dreams. Whom would I pick to play on my all-time, all-century, best-ever baseball team?

Let's start with the infield. My first baseman would be Lou Gehrig, the "Iron Horse" whose accomplishments made him an American hero and whose tragic early death made him a legend. Anyone playing with and batting behind Babe Ruth knew he had to park his ego in the clubhouse, but that was no problem for Lou. When he was asked what it was like to play in the Bambino's shadow, the Yankee first baseman replied, "It's a pretty big shadow. It gives me lots of room to spread myself."

The guy was a rock, which is why the late Jim Murray of the *Los Angeles Times* described him as a "Gibraltar in cleats." Before Cal Ripken came along, Gehrig played in 2,130 consecutive games until he became so weak that he could barely run out ground balls. After fourteen years of never missing a game, Lou pulled himself out of the lineup and checked himself into the Mayo Clinic early in the 1939 season. That's when Lou learned that he had a very rare form of degenerative disease called amyotrophic lateral sclerosis, or ALS. He lasted two years, dying at the age of thirty-seven. Today, the horrible affliction bears his name: Lou Gehrig's Disease, which is a fitting legacy.

My second baseman would be Jackie Robinson, the Dodger infielder who broke the color barrier in 1947. I know it's hard to contemplate, but for a long time Major League Baseball was a closed shop—only whites need apply. That was a shameful, absolutely shameful practice, and the abuse Jackie had to put up with during his rookie season—when he was under strict orders from his General

Manager Branch Rickey to *turn* the other cheek and *not* to retaliate—
would have broken any other mortal (see Chapter 48). I know I would
have snapped if I had been treated one day like he was. Jackie was
called the vilest names by fans, and bench jockeys from the other team
rode him for all he was worth. ("Hey, monkey, go back to the jungle"
was a typical epithet.) On the field, opposing players slid spikes up on
double-play balls, and pitchers knocked him down regularly. A *teammate*—Dixie Walker—even turned his head from the camera in
protest as the photographer snapped the official team photo of the
1947 Brooklyn Dodgers. That photo is on the cover of Harold Parrott's excellent book, *The Lords of Baseball.*

Still, Jackie endured and led the Dodgers to six pennants in ten
years. Twenty-five years after his death and fifty years after his break-
through, Major League Baseball retired No. 42 for every team in
both leagues in 1997. That was a great idea—long overdue but well-
deserved.

A-Rod is my man over at shortstop. I'm telling you, as a baseball fan it's a real treat to watch Alex Rodriguez play in his prime. We
should enjoy the way he is redefining an infield position while tearing up American League pitching. He's led the league in home runs,
RBIs, hitting average, doubles, grand slams, total bases, and runs
scored, although not in the same year, so he's a Triple Crown threat.
He was the first infielder to go "40/40"—forty home runs and forty
stolen bases.

I love A-Rod's all-business demeanor on the field and the way
he handles himself off the field. He will probably be acclaimed as
the greatest shortstop ever when he hangs 'em up.

My third baseman would be Mike Schmidt, who played the hot
corner for the Philadelphia Phillies when I was pitching. Most
people don't realize this, but Schmitty hit 548 home runs—only six
players have hit more. That guy has me in his book for five of them.
Mike owned me when I was pitching against him! A pure power hitter, Mike was also nimble around the third base bag, winning eleven

Gold Gloves and known for his bare-handed grabs of bunts. He always got the runner.

Now my starting outfield, although you may totally disagree with my selections because there are a dozen great players to choose from. But I only get to name three, so let me start with Ted Williams in left field. The "Splendid Splinter" was said to be the greatest pure hitter to have ever played the game. Williams's hitting prowess was such that visiting players crowded behind the batting cage whenever Ted stepped in because they wanted to learn from the maestro. It was said that his eyes were so good that he could follow the seams on the ball from the moment it left a pitcher's hand until he put wood on it—and could read the label on a 78 rpm record while it was spinning. (I know that 78 rpm record players had their heyday fifty years ago, but I'm told that platter spun really fast.) If Ted hadn't served his country in World War II *and* the Korean Conflict, he might have set career-hitting records that would still be standing today.

My favorite Ted Williams story is how he went out on a high note. On September 28, 1960, Ted played his final game for the Boston Red Sox at Fenway Park. Everyone knew this was it—the end of a long career that began in 1939. In his last at bat in the bottom of the eighth inning, Ted swung gracefully and met the pitch dead-on, driving a fastball 450 feet into the right center field seats behind the Boston bullpen.

I'm tapping Willie Mays as my center fielder, and you will not budge me off this pick. Willie was simply the most exciting player a fan could ever watch—you couldn't keep your eyes off him. Willie's most famous catch happened during the 1954 World Series against the Cleveland Indians. With the score 2–2 in the top of eighth inning at the Polo Grounds, Vic Wertz blasted a pitch deep into a spacious center field. Running full speed with his back to the infield, Willie sprinted toward the center field wall. With his glove extended over his left shoulder, he caught Wertz's ball 460 feet from home plate to save the game. Baseball historians refer to it simply as "The Catch." Willie had a way of making even routine fly balls fun to watch. If nobody was on base, he extended his arms in front of him and made a "basket catch" before tossing that can of corn back into the infield.

Willie was also a fearsome hitter who might have beaten Hank Aaron to Babe Ruth's home-run record if he hadn't played so many years in San Francisco's Candlestick Park, where prevailing winds off the bay blew home-run balls back into the waiting arms of opposing outfielders. We'll never know how many home runs Willie lost playing in the 'Stick, but he was still one of four players to pass the 600 home-run mark.

And starting in right field ... No. 44 ... Hank Aaron! I know that maybe you were thinking that I would name the great Babe Ruth, especially after reading elsewhere in this book that I refer to the Bambino as one of the greatest players ever. Maybe he was, but I have only three outfield spots open, and I have to look at this objectively. Hank Aaron was a better athlete and a better hitter than Babe Ruth. He began his career shortly after Jackie Robinson broke the color barrier, and when Hank retired in 1975, baseball was a fully integrated game pitting the very best athletes against each other. No slam against the Babe, but he played in a different era— train travel, fewer teams, all-white rosters. "Hammerin' Hank," meanwhile, hit more home runs than anyone else, and he passed the Babe under terrible adversity (he received numerous death threats that the FBI deemed credible). Some rednecks didn't want him to break the Babe's gold standard of 714 career home runs, but Hank did, and that's why he's on my team.

Now, you may be wondering, *Where's Barry Bonds?* Good question. In two or three years, Barry may eclipse Aaron's mark of 755 home runs, and the chatterboxes on ESPN *SportsCenter* will say that his face belongs on Mount Rushmore. When that happens, I will amend my starting outfield. Until that happens, however, I will say this: Barry Bonds was the greatest hitter I ever faced, and he is *the* dominant player of his generation and the greatest player of those still active. I'm fortunate that I faced him early in his career, before he had bulked up and started grooving that home-run swing of his. But I've got to find a place for him on my club, so give me this: Barry Bonds is my designated hitter when we play in American League parks.

I know I've left some great players off the starting lineup: Joe DiMaggio, Mickey Mantle, Ken Griffey Jr., Ty Cobb, Stan Musial, Roberto Clemente, Pete Rose, Joe Morgan, Don Drysdale, George Brett, Mark McGwire, and Yogi Berra. But I could only write one player's name on each line in my scorecard.

Let's turn our focus to my battery. Although I loved the way Terry Kennedy handled me when he was catching for the Padres, I know that Johnny Bench was the greatest player to squat behind the dish. Johnny, who was a mainstay with the Big Red Machine during the Cincinnati Reds' heyday in the 1970s, could field, hit, and throw out runners. He was also Mr. Endurance: he's the only catcher to play one hundred or more games for thirteen consecutive seasons.

Now I'm ready to name my starting pitchers. Nolan Ryan gets my call for right-handed pitcher. This fireballer could still bring the high heat into his early forties. For twenty-seven seasons that spanned four decades—that's unfathomable to me—Nolan challenged batters with a blistering fastball. The guy threw seven no-hitters and twelve one-hitters and became the all-time strikeout king with 5,714 punch-outs. That's ten times as many as me (I had 558 career K's). Nolan wasn't fazed taking the mound against anybody. He was the only pitcher to strike out the side on nine pitched balls in both the National League (April 19, 1968) and the American League (July 9, 1972).

Choosing my left-handed starter isn't as easy because the two guys I have warming up in the 'pen are Sandy Koufax and Randy Johnson. Sandy packed a Hall of Fame career into six seasons with the Los Angeles Dodgers in the early 1960s. The guy was practically unhittable, winning 119 games from 1961 to 1966 and three Cy Young awards.

Randy Johnson makes a strong claim as well, and the way he's still mowing them down, he may pitch well into his forties, just like the Ryan Express. The Big Unit has put up some big strikeout records (he's one of three pitchers to strike out twenty batters in a nine-inning game) and stingy ERA numbers.

But Sandy Koufax gets the ball. The reason I say that is that Mr. Koufax (I have that much respect for him) was my childhood idol. I was eight or nine years old when I started watching Sandy pitch on NBC's *Game of the Week*. Sandy, dressed in that classic Dodger uniform, would straddle the rubber at Chavez Ravine, then go into his windup as he uncoiled a high leg kick. I practiced and practiced that same leg kick when I pitched to my dad in our backyard. I wanted to be just like Sandy Koufax some day because I held him up on a huge pedestal.

I now realize the spiritual lesson to be learned here. I know that I'm choosing Mr. Koufax because I idolized him as a school kid. He was my pitching hero, and those feelings of looking up to him as a youngster have definitely influenced my decision to make him my starting pitcher. I think I chose Mr. Koufax because as a young boy, I read everything I could about him and tried to imitate him as best I could.

For us parents, that's a reminder of why it's important for youngsters to know about Jesus Christ from a young age. I can see it in my two children, Tiffany and Jonathan. They have known Jesus Christ since their kindergarten days, and that faith has strengthened over the years and gotten them through some tough times. They know how important it is to imitate Christ and to ask themselves, "What would Jesus do?"

When it came time for my children to make their relationship with Christ their own, they knew whom to call upon.

My Closer

It just occurred to me that I don't have a closer for the All-Time Dave Dravecky All-Stars. Now I feel a little better because I would like to tap Randy Johnson as my closer. At six feet, ten inches tall and the wingspan of a pterodactyl, Randy could stamp out any rally with his high heat. You want a guy who can strike batters out when there's men on base, and that is Randy's specialty.

For those of you who scoff at my selection, I would like to remind you that Randy came on in relief in Game 7 of the 2001 World Series between the Arizona Diamondbacks and the New York Yankees. Pitching with no day's rest, Randy kept the Yanks at bay with one-and-a-third innings of shutout ball before the Diamondbacks mounted an improbable bottom-of-ninth rally against feared closer Mariano Rivera.

So, Randy, stay loose until I need you.

They Said It

"Right now Andy Larkin is pitching just like a young Andy Larkin."

—Jerry Coleman, San Diego Padre radio announcer

FREEZER BURN   15

I have something more to say about one of my All-Stars—Ted Williams. Teddy Ball Game died in the summer of 2002 at the age of eighty-three. He lived a long time, was feted as the best hitter ever wherever he went, and earned way more money signing bats and balls—millions of dollars each year—than he ever did playing baseball.

I think all this talk about being immortal went to Ted's head—and to that of his son, John Henry Williams. Within hours after Ted's death of natural causes, John Henry shipped his father's lifeless body from Florida to a cryonics laboratory in Arizona, where he was embalmed with a glycerin-based solution and gradually lowered into a stainless steel tank of liquid nitrogen until his body reached a rather cool temperature of minus 320 degrees Fahrenheit. Later, according to *Sports Illustrated,* Williams's head was removed in "neuro-separation" surgery. In short, Ted Williams's separated head and body have been put on ice until his body parts can be defrosted and brought back to life—or perhaps cloned. Some have said that John Henry, who kept his dad busy signing memorabilia until he could no longer hold a Sharpie in his hand—wants to harvest the DNA for money.

The "Ted Williams jokes" started soon after Ted got colder than room temperature. Jay Leno on the *Tonight Show* said, "Ted Williams new rap name is 'Ice Cube.'" Another comic predicted that in the next baseball draft, Ted Williams's DNA would go in the first round. Baseball fans looking for a treat at the ballpark could choose from a Baby Ruth, Reggie Bar, or a Tedsicle. Or did you hear the joke about how Hannibal Lecter got brain freeze? Answer: from eating Ted Williams too quickly. *San Francisco Chronicle* columnist Scott Ostler said that when scientists find a way to bring the well-preserved back to life someday, we could see King Tut pitching against Ted Williams.

I know that this story is bizarre and beyond comprehension. It has pitted a son (John Henry Williams, by his third wife) who said his father wanted to be frozen against a daughter (Bobby-Jo Ferrell, from his first wife) who said that her father wanted his body cremated and his ashes spread over the Florida Keys, where he fished for years. What a mess! It was John Henry, however, who was calling the shots at the end of his father's life. He had taken control of his father's business affairs in the early 1990s, after he had washed out as a baseball player and had been hounded by creditors, causing him to file for bankruptcy. He and a second half sister, Claudia Williams, claimed that their father had signed a paper asking to be flash-frozen upon his death. "It's far from over," Claudia told one reporter. "He will live forever."

Oh, really? I guess I'm a purist—someone who expects U.S. Presidents to treat interns with respect and dead people to remain dead. Bobby-Jo Ferrell took her half brother and half sister to court, but six months after her father's death, she dropped her objections, saying that a legal fight would have cost her $250,000—money she didn't have. So she let it go. "We were whipped," said her husband, Mark.

Ted Williams was whipped as well when he died of old age—his heart gave out. His reflexes couldn't have been too quick, either. Let's just say that he couldn't turn on a fastball or read one of those labels on a 78 rpm record any longer. Even if Ted could be thawed in 3003, he'd still have to get around in a feeble, eighty-three-old body with a head reattached to his body. Then what? The whole thing doesn't make sense, including the basic premise of cryonics, which is the hope that science will one day have a cure for what killed you. Even if a cure for cancer were to be found, how would they bring someone back to life?

Let me remind the Williams family that only one man has died and rose again—Jesus Christ. (Yes, Lazarus came back from the dead in John 11, but Jesus, who alone has power over life and death, raised him from the dead. Moreover, Lazarus died again, but Jesus still lives.) After Christ's death on the cross, he could raise himself from the dead because he was—and is—God. He has always lived, and he will never die.

The human race has sought immortality and has been trying to cheat death for eons, but as Scripture reminds us in Hebrews 9:27, it is appointed unto man to die *once*. Not two times or three times, but once.

Not that this has kept the rich and powerful from trying. The pharaohs of Egypt built the pyramids—one of the Seven Wonders of the Ancient World—on the backs of tens of thousands of slaves and constructed elaborate mausoleums and even developed a remarkable system of embalming, all because they thought mummies could come back to life. The thirty-nine "Heaven's Gate" cultists who took their lives in 1997 did so because they thought they would catch a ride on a spaceship trailing the Hale-Bopp Comet—and live happily ever after.

Christians take a different route to immortality. By trusting in Jesus Christ as our Savior, we are promised eternal life with him in heaven. That promise comes from someone who *really* cheated death. Remember, the Bible states that more than five hundred people saw Jesus after he rose on the third day and before he ascended into heaven. The Resurrection really happened, and it's the linchpin of our faith. If Jesus didn't conquer death, then he was not who he said he was—the Son of God.

I'm glad that I've found what I'm looking for. I just wonder if Ted ever found the same Prince of Peace.

Stairway to Heaven

Two old guys, Abe and Sol, sat on a park bench, feeding pigeons and talking about baseball, just as they did every day. Abe turned to Sol and said, "Do you think there's baseball in heaven?"

Sol thought about it for a minute and replied, "I dunno. But let's make a deal. If I die first, I'll come back and tell you if there's baseball in heaven. And if you die first, you do the same."

They shook on it but sadly, a few months later, poor Abe passed on. One day soon afterward, Sol was sitting on the park bench by himself, feeding the pigeons, when he heard a voice whisper, "Sol . . . Sol . . ."

"Abe! Is that you?"

"Yes, it is, Sol," whispered Abe's ghost.

Sol, still amazed, asked, "So, is there baseball in heaven?"

"Well," said Abe, "I've got some good news and some bad news."

"Gimme the good news first," said Sol.

"Well, there is baseball in heaven."

"That's great!" Sol exclaimed. "What news could be bad enough to ruin that?"

Abe sighed. "You're pitching on Friday."

They Said It

"If manager Pete Rose brings the Reds into first place, they ought to bronze him and put him in cement."

—Jerry Coleman, San Diego Padre radio announcer

MY BIG FAT GREEK MIRACLE 16

I don't know whether you've seen pictures of me lately, but I'm definitely not at my playing weight of 210 pounds. Try something like thirty pounds north of that. It's tough losing weight when you're in your mid-forties, can't exercise like you used to, and speak at luncheons and dinners where they serve mounds of delicious food.

That's why the story of Dr. Nick Yphantides (pronounced Eee-fahn-tee-dees) is so inspirational to me. Finally, here is a man after my own heart—actually, stomach. It seems that Dr. Nick, a family physician from Escondido, California—about thirty miles north of San Diego—had this weight problem. He kept eating and eating until he ballooned to 467 pounds.

As the son of Greek immigrants and a family physician, Dr. Nick Yphantides was known as a larger-than-life advocate for the poor, the big man with a big heart who cared for his community in a big way. Overweight patients *loved* Dr. Nick because they knew they would receive tea and sympathy from someone who also shopped at Mr. Big and Tall.

But as Nick turned thirty years old, he began experiencing declining health and a host of unusual symptoms that led him to a doctor's examination room. A week later, he learned the bad news: Nick had testicular cancer.

The surgical excision of the right testicle and aggressive radiation over twelve weeks saved his life—and caused some soul-searching. The way Nick saw it, he had dodged the cancer bullet, but there was another round in the chamber: his gargantuan weight had to be causing incredible amounts of stress on his organs—heart, lungs, and liver, as well as his skeletal frame. He wondered how much stress he was putting on his knees, which were bearing such a severe load.

One day, Nick stood on two scales—one for each foot. The digital readout said "233.5." A third-grader could do the math: Dr. Nick Yphantides, the jolly doc with the Santa Claus–like image around town, weighed in at a hefty 467 pounds. Nick was scared. His cancer had forced him to face his mortality, and now he was sure that each bite of a juicy double cheeseburger brought him one swallow closer to the grave.

Something needed to be done. Nick was tired of dressing in XXXXL T-shirts and tent-sized gym pants, tired of booking uncrowded red-eye flights so that he wouldn't have to buy a second seat, tired of gawkers staring at his monstrous midsection in restaurants. Ahead of him was a future filled with high blood pressure, high cholesterol, and debilitating diabetes—unless he made some radical lifestyle changes and lost a ton of weight. Well, maybe not a ton, but two hundred pounds would be a good start, he figured.

Nick began formulating a game plan. He needed to step away from work and concentrate on losing weight. He also needed something to do—a diversion to keep his mind off being so hungry. That's it! Nick loved baseball—he was a Padres season ticket holder—so he decided to drive around the country and visit every major league ballpark while watching baseball games. To lose weight slowly but surely, he would embark on a liquid fast—drinking a protein supplement offering just eight hundred calories a day. As a physician, he knew that this type of aggressive diet had to be medically monitored along the way.

On April 1, 2001, Nick sailed off in a used Chevy van conversion—a vehicle he christened the *USS Spirit of Reduction*—with the intention of becoming half the man he used to be. His father, George, rode shotgun. Going cold turkey from food gave Nick the shakes, just like any junkie coming down off a high. He was so hungry that he would have eaten a cigarette butt dipped in mustard, he said.

Two cities known for their gastronomical delights were particularly painful to visit: Kansas City, for its butter-fried steaks; and New Orleans, for its Cajun-style fish and shrimp. At times the only thing that kept him going, he said, was knowing that hundreds of people back home had pledged varying amounts of money for every pound he lost—money that would go to the Escondido Community Health Center and the California Center for the Arts. That unique accountability contributed toward helping Nick accomplish the goal he set.

Some amazing things happened while he was on his 38,000-mile odyssey. One afternoon, Nick was minding his business as he watched Sammy Sosa and the Chicago Cubs take on the Colorado Rockies in the "friendly confines" of Wrigley Field. Suddenly, on a hot, humid August afternoon, a woman three rows behind Nick jumped up and started screaming that her mother had passed out.

"I jumped over several rows of seats, and when I got to the woman, she was lifeless," Nick said. "There was no pulse, and she wasn't breathing. She had gone into cardiac arrest. I laid her down and started CPR, and on the third cycle, she started breathing again."

Paramedics arrived a few minutes later and whisked the woman to the hospital, but the Wrigley Field crowd knew a good play when they saw it: they stood and gave Dr. Nick a standing ovation, which he acknowledged with the doff of a hat.

A few weeks later, Nick was in his old hometown of Ridgefield, New Jersey, arriving on the night of September 10, 2001, at some family member's house.

The next morning, his grandfather burst into his bedroom. "Hey, Nick, you gotta see this!"

Scenes of a United Airlines Flight 175 flying dead-on into the south tower of the World Trade Center were being replayed as both towers smoldered in fire and smoke.

After the towers collapsed, Nick called his office in Escondido and asked them to fax his medical credentials. Then he took off for New York City to offer his medical services. Like many other doctors who volunteered that fateful day, Nick was not needed because so few people survived the collapse of the World Trade Center towers.

His persistence was rewarded two days later, however. "I visited an armory where many of the victims' families had gathered," he said. "I offered what counseling and aid I could."

He returned to San Diego following the 2001 World Series (which he attended in New York *and* Phoenix) two hundred and thirty pounds lighter, which amazed his mother and siblings. At Thanksgiving, nieces and nephews didn't even recognize him at a family reunion. He ate his first solid food in nearly eight months on Thanksgiving Day—some vegetables and a baked potato.

The end of his long weight-loss trip was just a beginning, Nick learned. Now he would have to work at keeping the pounds off. He eased back into his practice, working just twenty hours a week at the clinic and seeing child victims of abuse. That freed up a chunk of time to exercise; these days he spends an average of three hours at a YMCA fast-walking a treadmill and pumping iron. Today, he weighs close to my old baseball weight—210 pounds, which means he's lost more than 250 pounds.

Nick made a long-term goal and stuck to it. What an inspiration he is to the rest of us. I like his idea about traveling around the country watching baseball games—but not eat at the ballpark?

Now that's an amazing stat.

A Way to Go

Dr. Nick's experience with the heart attack victim at Wrigley Field reminds me of another story, but this one doesn't have the same happy ending.

This story begins during my rookie year with the Padres in 1982. The parent club had called me up, and you can only imagine how excited I was to be part of The Show. I circled the date of my calendar marking our first road trip to Cincinnati, around three hundred miles from Youngstown, Ohio, my hometown. I knew that a couple of dozen family members and friends couldn't wait to see me play at Riverfront Stadium.

We opened with a doubleheader against the Reds. I was a reliever in those days, sitting in the bullpen and spitting sunflower seeds into the dirt until something happened. In the seventh inning, the phone rang. "Dravecky, warm up," barked my pitching coach, Norm Sherry. I grabbed my glove, took off my light jacket, and walked toward the bullpen mound. I was excited for two reasons: one, I was still looking for my first major league save; and two, my family and friends were on hand to watch me play for the first time.

I tossed the ball at half-speed to my bullpen catcher. Out of the corner of my eye, I noticed some commotion in the stands behind the Padre dugout. It looked like paramedics had been called to the scene. "Man, I hope whoever got hurt is okay," I said to my catcher.

I returned to the task at hand, but the Red threat passed and I sat down again. The same thing happened in the second game of the twinbill: I warmed up in the bullpen, but I didn't get to go in.

When the long day at the ballpark was over, I jogged toward the clubhouse. "Dave, can I talk to you a moment?" asked Norm Sherry, who pulled me over to the side.

"Sure, Coach. What's happening?"

"Dave, I'm afraid I have some bad news to report," he said.

The color drained from my face. Was I being sent down already?

"Remember how you were warming up in the first game and there was all that commotion in the stands?"

"Yeah, I remember."

"Well, it seems that your mother-in-law had a heart attack."

I was shocked. "Is she—"

He nodded his head. She was gone.

Later, my dad described what happened. After I had gotten up to warm up in the first game, Jan's mom, Lacea, asked my father if he thought I would come into the game. Then she fell backward in her seat. Just like that, she was gone—dead from a heart attack.

It fell upon my shoulders to call Jan back in San Diego, where she was caring for our baby Tiffany. That was one sad phone call.

I thought it was strange that no one told me what happened during the game, but there was nothing I could have done. I know I couldn't have pitched if I *had* known because games don't seem very important when compared to life-and-death issues.

I take solace in three things about Lacea's death:

1. She knew the Lord, so she went on to her heavenly reward with Jesus.
2. She died quickly, which can be a tremendous blessing.
3. She died while watching a Major League baseball game.

That's not a bad way to go. It's just a shame that she had to leave us so soon.

They Said It

> *"Well, that kind of puts a damper on another Yankee win."*

—New York Yankee announcer Phil Rizzuto after a news bulletin announced the unexpected death of Pope Paul VI

TAKE ME OUT TO THE BANK BEFORE YOU TAKE ME OUT TO THE BALL GAME

17

What does it cost a family of four to go to the old ballpark these days?

Around $150, when you factor in the price of four mid-range tickets, a program, four hotdogs, four Cokes, four ice creams, and some peanuts and Cracker Jack. That's a lot of coin, but I still think that baseball is the best buy in town, especially when you compare it to the cost of taking a family to an NHL hockey game (around $300), an NBA basketball game ($325), or an NFL football game (around $325). And that doesn't include parking.

So at half the price, baseball is a bargain, and it should be. With a six-game-a-week schedule, baseball games are like a street trolley—if you miss one, there's another coming right up. Still, we have to face things squarely on and recognize that $150 is a lot of money to the average family, and prices have risen dramatically in the last five years—for all the major sports. Seats that were $16 are now $24; $20 seats are now $32—that kind of thing.

Did you know that ticket prices go up an average of 35 percent when the home team moves into a new ballpark? Since 1990, two-thirds of the thirty major league teams moved into new ballparks, but many of these old-style "retro" fields have been constructed in the last five years or so. In fact, ten of the sixteen National League teams play in parks built in 1997 or later. Closer to home, my Giants moved into Pacific Bell Park in 2000 and received rave reviews for its breathtaking views, classic design, and McCovey's Cove just beyond the right field bleachers. And with the start of the 2004 season, my Padres will be playing in spiffy new downtown digs called Petco Park. Other new parks include:

- Philadelphia's Phillies Citizens Bank Park (opening in 2004)
- Cincinnati's Great American Ball Park (opened in 2003)
- Milwaukee's Miller Park (opened in 2001)
- Pittsburgh's PNC Park (opened in 2001)
- Houston's Minute Maid Park (originally christened Enron Field when it opened in 2000)
- Phoenix's Bank One Ballpark (opened in 1998)
- Atlanta's Turner Field (opened in 1997)
- Colorado's Coors Field (opened in 1995)

If that wasn't enough, St. Louis will have a new ballpark for the 2005 season, and there are plans on the board to construct new ballparks in Miami, Montreal, and New York City (for the Mets). The American League isn't being left behind either. New ballparks include:

- Detroit's Comerica Park (opened in 2000)
- Seattle's Safeco Field (opened in 1999)
- Anaheim's Edison International Field (completely renovated in 1998)
- Cleveland's Jacobs Field (opened in 1994)
- Texas' The Ballpark at Arlington (opened in 1994)
- Baltimore's Oriole Park at Camden Yards (opened in 1994)
- Chicago's U.S. Cellular Field (opened as the New Comiskey Park in 1991)
- Tampa Bay's Tropicana Field (opened in 1990)

A little more than half of the fourteen American League teams are playing in stadiums built since 1990, but plans are kicking around to replace Fenway Park, Yankee Stadium, and the Metrodome.

As I mentioned before, new ballparks mean the owners can announce new pricing. What baseball—and the other major sports—has discovered is that corporations that buy luxury suites and field-level season tickets are fairly price-insensitive when it comes to renewing. The corporate suits love entertaining clients in the luxury suites ringing the baselines, so they will fork over hundreds of thousands of dollars a year to buy one. In addition, single-game sales have been helped by the rising disposable income of higher-income families, who have demonstrated a willingness to pay any price for a night at the ballpark.

If there is a silver lining, it's that the cheap seats are still, well, cheap. Nosebleed seats in the upper deck and way back in the outfield are often under ten bucks. Then there are the "specials" that baseball clubs run during off-peak times, just like the airlines. Thursday games—played early in the afternoon so that the visiting club can fly to the next destination in time for a Friday night start—are called "Businessman Specials," although in some precincts, the PC-friendly term is "Businessperson Special." Either way, some clubs offer two-for-one discounts on tickets since most people have to work during the day (Don't you hate when that happens?).

The San Diego Padres offer a twenty-buck special for families on Monday nights—another dead spot on the schedule. For just one Andrew Jackson, a family of four receives four bleacher seats, four hot dogs, and four sodas. That's a great deal for five dollars a head.

Now, in the interest of full disclosure, I must tell you that I can go see *any* game I want for free by showing a special pass I received from Bill White, the National League president at the time I had to retire back in 1989.

Here's what happened. After enduring cancer surgery on my left arm, I made my miraculous comeback with the San Francisco Giants. Everything was going great until my left arm snapped in two, ending my career. Within a year, doctors had to amputate my left arm at the shoulder.

During my recuperation, I received a thoughtful get-well note from Bill White. Accompanying the letter was a "golden pass," good for admission to any major league baseball game for the rest of my life. Every player who plays ten seasons receives such a pass, but I was part of The Show for only seven years and 116 days. I didn't deserve the free pass.

Bill White noted that the golden pass was only distributed to players with ten years of service, but because of the situation with losing my arm and all, he thought receiving it would boost my spirits.

That is so much like how God treats us. He's willing to give us a golden pass to heaven when we have done nothing to deserve it.

The funny thing is that I only go to two, maybe three games a season these days. Coors Field is sixty miles north of my home in Colorado Springs, so it's not terribly convenient to go. You might say that I take the golden pass for granted.

But I don't, because I know I'll always have it. It's the same way with my salvation. I have *that* golden pass tucked away in a safe place, and I'll only have to show it once upon entrance to a place far greater than all the baseball palaces being built today.

Mark of the Beast

You could say that John Rocker had a rocky career, but at one time, he sure had the baseball world by the tail. When he was pitching for the Atlanta Braves in the late 1990s, the hard-throwing left-handed closer charged out of bullpens and blew away batters with ease.

It's too bad his pinpoint control didn't extend to his mouth. The Braves pitcher made some ill-advised comments about homosexuals and New York City's colorful ethnic population, and suddenly everyone wanted his scalp. Then he had what armchair psychologists would call "anger issues." John Rocker was mad at the world, and it showed.

Perhaps it's fitting that John's 2002 season with the Texas Rangers ended with a hellish number: poor JR finished with a 6.66 ERA.

Now that's a revelation, wouldn't you say?

They Said It

"Take Me Out to the Corporate-Sponsored Megaplex."

—Dave Letterman, offering his idea to modernize baseball's seventh-inning stretch song

BIG BROTHER IS WATCHING   18

Have you heard about QuesTec?

Major league umpires certainly have. More than a dozen major league ball clubs have installed the QuesTec Umpire Information System, which uses computerized tracking info to determine if a pitch is in the hitter's strike zone. Many baseball executives believe that QuesTec can call balls and strikes better than the umps can. If true, the implications are enormous.

Can you imagine the catcher sitting in his usual crouch, wig-wagging signs, and then putting out his big mitt to receive the pitch—without an umpire looking over his shoulder? I know the thought boggles the mind, and I hope it never happens since I'm a traditionalist. Even someone like me, who's yelled, "Kill the ump" occasionally, wouldn't want the QuesTec system to make the home-plate umpire as extinct as the dodo bird.

Actually, no-umps-at-home-plate will never happen since you would still need an ump to call foul tips, judge whether bunts stay fair, and call "safe" or "out" on a tag play at the plate. But QuesTec is making more than a few umps sweat because it provides digital proof that each ump has his own strike zone—and that the zone widens or shrinks as the game moves along. The people in charge of umpiring for Major League Baseball have been using QuesTec to evaluate their performances, which can affect postseason assignments or contract offers that the umps get the following year.

Here's how the system works. Four cameras put in strategic places in the stadium record a video of the batter, and a technician sets each batter's strike zone. Then software merges data from all four cameras to show the position of the ball as it passes over the plate. The results speak as clearly as a pitch splitting the heart of the plate.

The umps get it right about 90 percent of the time, which infuriates the umpiring fraternity. Ninety percent is very good, but umps are expected to be perfect. They have attacked the science behind QuesTec and filed grievances with Major League Baseball and the National Labor Relations Board.

Baseball executives are saying all they want is a uniform strike zone and that umpires shouldn't run home plate like a personal fiefdom where their personal strike zone can be anything they want it to be.

So what will it be—man or machine?

I'll take the ump any day. So what if they don't call every pitch right? That's part of the beauty of the game. Besides, I can't imagine anyone but the man in blue punching out the batter on a called third strike. What fun is it arguing with a machine anyway?

They Said It

"We're supposed to be perfect our first day on the job, and then show constant improvement."

—Ed Vargo, Major League Baseball umpire

A LOOK AT THE BABE

No man had more nicknames on earth than George Herman Ruth:

The Babe
The Man
The Bambino
The Home-Run King
The Circuit Smasher
The Colossus of Clout
Herman the Great
The Mauler
The Bustin' Bambino
And finally, my all-time favorite, the Sultan of Swat

He picked up his signature nickname shortly after Jack Dunn, owner of the Baltimore Orioles minor league team, signed the then nineteen-year-old Ruth to a contract for the princely sum of a hundred dollars a month. That's a sum far less than what today's players receive per diem for food and taxis! A pitcher in those days, the young Ruth must have looked like a busher because when he and Dunn walked to the mound on the first day of spring training, someone hollered, "Look at Dunnie and his new babe."

Babe Ruth he became. It's hard for us to imagine how famous the Bambino became in the 1920s and 1930s. Built with the pug nose of a fighter and a stevedore's barrel chest, Babe stood on pipestem legs and swung for the fences. When one of his monstrous blasts cleared the wall, he circled the bases in those mincing steps before receiving a handshake from teammate Lou Gehrig.

Probably half the stories written about him were exaggerations, and the other half were outright false. It was said that he had been born an orphan and raised by Jesuit priests, that he once ate half a dozen sandwiches and an entire jar of pig's knuckles before leaving the clubhouse and hitting a six-hundred-foot homer, and that the Yankees adopted pinstripes to make Ruth appear slimmer. It's highly doubtful that any of those stories are true. Besides, the Yanks were already playing in pinstripes when he arrived from Boston.

That didn't stop sportswriters from writing reams of copy about his hitting exploits and huge appetite. The nationwide interest in Babe Ruth turned him into a larger-than-life character. During the 1920s, his name appeared in print more often than anyone except for the president of the United States. When it was learned that he was paid more than President Herbert Hoover in 1930, earning $80,000 to the President's $75,000, the Babe quipped, "But I had a better year than Hoover."

Ruth was so famous that years later during World War II, when American GIs shouted "To hell with the Emperor!" at Japanese soldiers, the ones who could speak English yelled back, "To hell with Babe Ruth!"

Now that was a low blow.

As big as Babe Ruth was as a player and a personality, his glittering assortment of nicknames doesn't come close to portraying the grace and majesty of the names we have for Christ. Bible scholars have scoured Scripture and found nearly *six hundred* references to Christ ranging from "The Advocate" to "The Zeal of the Lord of Hosts."

Some of my favorites are:

- The Alpha and the Omega
- The Bread of Life
- The Good Shepherd
- The King of Kings
- The Lamb of God
- The Savior
- The Son of Man
- The Teacher

Leave it to the Lord of Lords to smash the record book on names.

A Heck of a Hex

During the 2003 American League Championship Series and National League Championship Series, we sure heard a lot about the "Curse of the Bambino" on the Boston Red Sox and the "billy goat curse" put on the Chicago Cubs.

I don't take any stock in curses, but even I have to shake my head in disbelief at how the Red Sox and the Cubs snatched defeat from the jaws of victory during the 2003 playoffs. Both teams had three-run leads in the eighth inning and were just five outs from going to the World Series when they suddenly couldn't get anyone out. The way both clubs imploded on national TV was eerie and sad since most casual fans were pulling for a World Series between the Red Sox and the Cubs.

The actual "curses" on these two clubs have taken a life of their own. If you're not from the Northeast, then you may be unfamiliar with the "Curse of the Bambino." Here's how the story goes: Ever since Red Sox owner Harry Frazee sold Babe Ruth to the New York Yankees for $100,000 following the 1919 season, Boston hasn't won a World Series. That's eighty-five years of futility, supposedly caused because the Red Sox sold the greatest player of all time like some sort of cheap chattel.

You can certainly argue that the balance of power shifted after Babe Ruth began wearing No. 3 in Yankee pinstripes. Prior to 1919, the Red Sox won five world championships and the Yanks none. Everyone knows what's happened since the 1920s: the Yankees became symbols of American domination by winning twenty-six World Series championships, the most of any team in any professional sport. As for the Boston Red Sox, they qualified for post-season play nine times but never won the big one.

They've certainly come achingly close. The Red Sox battled the Yankees to a Game 7 in the 2003 playoffs and handed their pitching ace, Pedro Martinez, a three-run lead going into the eighth inning.

That's when a rain of hits made up the deficit, and a Yankee comeback was capped when light-hitting Aaron Boone launched a rainbow-like home run in the eleventh inning to seal New York's improbable victory.

For Red Sox fans, that loss was a bitter one to swallow, and it dredges up memories of the 1986 World Series against the New York Mets. Boston had grabbed a 3–2 series lead, and they were leading the Mets in the ninth inning of Game 6. The Red Sox had New York down to its final strike when weird things started to happen. Mookie Wilson of the Mets dribbled a ground ball toward first baseman Bill Buckner. It was a routine play that Buckner had fielded 10,000 times cleanly before—but the ball squirted between his legs, costing the Red Sox Game 6 and eventually the Series.

Although sportswriters had a field day blaming the "Curse of the Bambino" to explain what happened on the playing field, there was no curse. The Red Sox lost to the Mets in 1986 and to the Yankees in 2003 because their pitchers couldn't get anyone out when it counted and players in the field committed errors.

Over the years, though, a few of the Beantown faithful have tried to get rid of the Ruth jinx. Babe Ruth, it was said, had rented a small lake house on Willis Pond—about an hour's drive from Boston— when he was playing for the Red Sox. One night, a drunken Ruth was playing a small upright but out-of-tune piano in the home. He became so enraged that he pitched the piano into the lake. Another legend has it that a wintertime party got out of hand, and the revelers pushed the piano onto the frozen pond to have a good time. They left the piano there until the spring thaw, when the waters claimed it.

It's doubtful that either of those scenarios happened, but that hasn't stopped some Red Sox fans from coming up with a *Field of Dreams*–like brainstorm: *If we can find it, then he (and his curse) will leave.* In other words, if they could find the piano in Willis Pond after all these years, the curse would be lifted and the Red Sox would win the World Series. People really believe this. In fact, two Red Sox fans,

Kevin Kennedy and Eloise Newell, organized a search of Willis Pond a couple of years ago. A friend dragged an infrared camera behind a skiff, and a volunteer dive team poked around the muddy bottom.

Their "ruthless" quest has yet to be rewarded. I realize this search for Babe Ruth's piano is the product of well-intentioned people with too much time on their hands, but do you think God would allow the ghost of Babe Ruth, as it has been called, to determine the fate of the Boston Red Sox? If I can turn serious for a moment, we are warned in Scripture not to have anything to do with ghosts or spirits or divination: "No Israeli may practice black magic, or call on the evil spirits for aid, or be a fortune teller, or be a serpent charmer, medium, or wizard, or *call forth the spirits of the dead*" (Deuteronomy 18:10, TLB, with italics added for emphasis).

Even if Babe Ruth's piano were to be found in the muck of Willis Pond, that wouldn't change anything. Someday, the Boston Red Sox will win the World Series. It may not be in my lifetime, and it may not be in yours, but it will happen someday. You have to be a realist. It's tough to win it all today because thirty teams are trying to do the same thing and New York Yankee owner George Steinbrenner buys up all the great players, just like his predecessor Jacob Rupert did when he purchased Babe Ruth in 1919.

Some people don't like to face that truth.

Those Cursed Cubs

The way the Chicago Cubs lost to the Florida Marlins in the 2003 National League Championship Series was bizarre. The Cubbies disintegrated in Game 6 after Cub fan Steve Bartman reached for a foul ball when Cub leftfielder Moises Alou had a play on the ball. (By the way, the foul ball was barely in the stands, so it wasn't fan interference. Like Bartman said afterward, if he had known Alou could have caught the ball, he would have let a member of his favorite team make the catch.)

Yeah, it was too bad the Cubs blew three straight games to the Marlins, but they had three chances to get to the World Series. I was really pulling for the Cubbies because they're usually knocked out of the pennant chase by Mother's Day.

Commentators and sportswriters blamed the loss to the Marlins on the "billy goat curse," and here's the story on that. It seems that William Sianis, a Greek immigrant, opened up a bar on Michigan Avenue in 1934 and called it the Billy Goat Tavern. Sianis was born with a bum leg and a knack for self-promotion. He made his tavern a second home to the ink-stained wretches of the Fourth Estate—the writers on the *Chicago Tribune, Chicago-Sun Times,* and a host of smaller papers. They, in turn, helped make the Billy Goat Tavern the most popular bar in the Windy City.

Perhaps it was with an eye for publicity that caused Bill Sianis to bring his pet billy goat with him to Wrigley Field during the 1945 World Series when the Cubbies were playing the Detroit Tigers. Sianis had two tickets in his hand—one for him, and one for his goat named Murphy. The bar owner had purchased a separate ticket for the goat in Box 65, Tier 12, Seat 5.

He talked his way through the ticket-taker at the turnstile, but an usher put his foot down, saying that the goat stank up the joint. Sianis stormed out of Wrigley, vowing to put a hex on the team.

Years later, someone told Cubs owner P. K. Wrigley about the hex—it was probably one of the boozy writers who occupied a Billy Goat Tavern barstool every afternoon—prompting the owner to write a letter in 1950 asking Sianis to lift the curse and extend his heartfelt apologies to Murphy.

Forgettaboutit, Sianis replied. *Besides, my pet billy goat died of a broken heart.*

Here's where the story takes a twist. Years pass by, and the Cubbies finally have a good team in 1969. Manager Leo Durocher has the club out in front by nine games in August, everyone in Chicago is excited, and Bill Sianis graciously "lifts" the curse—and gets more publicity for his tavern.

But the Cubs collapse and don't make it back to the World Series. A year later, Sianis dies.

Ah, but a nephew named Sam takes over the family business. During the 1973 season, the Cubs are hot again—leading the NL Eastern Division by seven games on the Fourth of July. Amid all the hoopla, Sam decides to bring his pet goat Socrates into Wrigley Field that day, but the ushers kick him out. So Sam puts the "curse" back on. Two weeks later, the Cubs fall from their lofty first-place perch.

When the Tribune Co. purchased the Cubs in 1982 from the Wrigley estate, they decided to make peace with the Curse of the Billy Goat. Socrates was invited as the special guest on Opening Day, and Sam announced that the curse was off.

I can remember that stupid old billy goat being in the news when we (by that, I mean the San Diego Padres) played the Cubs for the National League pennant in 1984. It was best-of-five back then, with the first two games at Wrigley Field. Socrates was an invited dignitary, and he must have sewn his wild oats after watching the Cubs pound us for five home runs in a 13–0 rout in Game 1. Game 2 was closer in the "friendly confines," but we lost 4–2. I made my first postseason appearance, pitching one inning and giving up no runs. Still, we lost, and now our backs were firmly against the wall.

On the plane ride back to San Diego, Goose Gossage, our closer and team leader, said, "Guys, look—don't sweat this. Yeah, we've lost two, but we can't change that. What we *can* do is take the next game. So let's just think about that—winning one game at a time. And you pitchers, especially those coming out of the bullpen, be thinking about making one pitch at a time. Let's keep our ball club close enough to give us an opportunity to win."

Our skipper, Dick Williams, told us that he would need a total team effort, especially from the pitching staff. "I'm going to have a quick hook," said the Padre manager. "We need everyone ready to give us 100 percent, whether it's for one batter or one inning or a complete game. Be ready."

Four thousand fans were waiting for us at Lindbergh Field when we landed at 2:30 in the morning, cheering us like crazy. That lifted our spirits. We climbed back into the series by winning Game 3. I got to see some action in Game 4 when I shut out the Cubs in the sixth and seventh innings, setting the table for Goose and Craig Lefferts. We had caught the Cubs.

I will never forget the deciding Game 5. The Cubs broke out to a 3–0 lead, but we manufactured two runs in the sixth to pull within one. Then some wacky stuff happened. Tim Flannery squirted a ground ball toward Chicago's first baseman Leon Durham, who charged only to watch the ball scoot between his legs. (It was the same type of grounder that Bill Buckner of the Red Sox would boot two years later.) Then Alan Wiggins pitched a soft wedge shot in front of left fielder Gary Matthews, putting runners on first and second. Tony Gwynn lined a one-hopper toward Ryne Sandberg at second base, but the ball struck something and took a crazy hop over Sandberg. Two runs scored. Steve Garvey then finished the scoring parade with a run-scoring single, giving the Padres a 6–3 lead. Goose shut 'em down the rest of the way, and the Padres capped an improbable but historic comeback.

Now let me attempt to bring this story full circle. We were talking about the Curse of the Billy Goat that lay on the Chicago Cubs. Some of the Chicago faithful noted that since Socrates didn't make the trip to San Diego, that is why we ran the table and took San Diego to its first World Series. They have it all wrong. We won, and the Cubs didn't. The series was decided on the field of play, just as it was against the Florida Marlins in 2003. Believe me, no one on the Padre bench or the Marlin bench was thinking about that stupid goat. We knew skill, determination, and a lucky bounce or two determined the games. *And that's how every game is played!*

Here's how I deal with a bad hop or bad luck in life: I don't worry about it. What's done is done. God is in control, and he will always be in control, and anything we do to try to understand why some things happen will be fraught with frustration. "'My thoughts are completely different from yours,' says the LORD. 'And my ways are far beyond anything you could imagine. For just as the heavens are higher than the earth, so are my ways higher than your ways and my thoughts higher than your thoughts'" (Isaiah 55:8–9, NLT).

I'm glad he has it all figured out.

They Said It

"I heard Billy Buckner tried to commit suicide over the winter. He stepped in front of a car, but it went through his legs."

—Billy Gardner, Kansas City Royals manager

THE CURSE ON THE ANGELS   20

Let's talk about another curse—but this one got laid to rest during the 2002 World Series.

I'm talking about the curse surrounding the Anaheim Angels. Remember those stories that came out when the Angels were making their stretch run and trying to make it into the World Series? This time the writers weren't saying that the Angels had to win the World Series to beat the Curse—they merely had to *get* to the World

Series to lay the Curse to rest. To prove their point, the columnists catalogued the dreadful things that had happened to the team and players over the years:

- In 1965, rookie pitcher Dick Wantz died of a brain tumor.
- In 1968, reliever Minnie Rojas was paralyzed in an auto accident that killed his wife and two of their three children.
- In 1972, second baseman Chico Ruiz was killed in a car crash.
- In 1974, rookie reliever Bruce Heinbechner died in a car crash.
- In 1974, Mike Miley was killed in a car crash.
- In 1978, Lyman Bostock, an MVP-type talent, was struck by a bullet while riding in a car—a bullet meant for his passenger. He died.
- In 1982, the Angels became the first team to blow a 2–0 lead in a five-game League Championship Series, dropping three in a row to the Milwaukee Brewers.
- In 1986, the Angels took a commanding 3–1 lead in a best-of-seven series against the Boston Red Sox and had a 5–2 lead into the ninth inning of Game 5. Closer Donnie Moore, working with a two-out and 2–2 count—one strike away from the World Series—surrendered a home run that cost the Angels the game, and ultimately the American League Championship Series.
- In 1989, Donnie Moore shot himself to death, unable to cope with throwing a home-run ball to Boston's Dave Henderson.
- In 1999, first baseman Mo Vaughn—two batters into the new season—chased after a foul ball and fell into the visitor's dugout, severely spraining his ankle. Vaughn missed twenty-three games and played on a sore ankle all season.

Granted, I've listed some mystifying losses, horrible tragedies, and weird injuries, and I can especially relate to the despondency that Donnie Moore experienced because I battled depression myself after I lost my left arm and my baseball career in one fell swoop of the doctor's knife. But the Angels were no more cursed than I was. Stuff happens, as the bumper sticker says.

Until they got into the 2002 World Series against Barry Bonds and the San Francisco Giants, however, many people in the Angels organization thought they had run afoul of the spirits. As the car crashes and tragedies took their toll over the years, someone told owner Gene Autry—the "Singing Cowboy"—that Anaheim Stadium, as it was called back in the 1960s, was built atop an ancient Indian burial ground—and that was the reason for the curse. No one ever proved this, but after hearing friends and people tell him for twenty years that his team was cursed because of this, Autry bought into it.

Jackie Autry, his wife, said after Gene's death that her husband had looked into getting the clubhouse exorcised and discussed burying his ashes beneath home plate so as to ward off the bad vibes of the Indian burial ground.

Thankfully, Autry's cremated ashes were disposed of elsewhere, and thankfully too, the "Curse of the Angels" has been finally laid to rest.

They Said It

"Even Napoleon had his Watergate."

—Danny Ozark, Philadelphia Phillies manager, commenting on the team's ten-game losing streak

One of my favorite sayings in the Bible comes from Galatians 6:7 (NLT): "Don't be misled. Remember that you can't ignore God and get away with it. You will always reap what you sow!"

That verse came to mind when I saw the news that my Padres had eleven players in their Minor League system playing under false names and ages. The Padre organization stumbled on the deception by accident. After the U.S. Immigrations and Naturalization Service issued stricter rules regarding validation of visa information in the wake of September 11, the Padre front office ran a check of their foreign players. Identity switching was rampant:

- Jackson Aquino was actually Alsenio De La Cruz and two years, two months older.
- Luis Bereguete was actually Alexander Garcia and one year, ten months older.
- Pedro De Los Santos was actually Freddy Guzman and two years, six months older.
- Jhovany Espinal was actually Geivy Garcia and one year, nine months older.
- Angleidy Garcia was actually Domingo Martinez and three years, eight months older.
- Elvin Moya was Gabriel Moya and one year, nine months older.
- Johan Paulino was actually George Vasquez and two years, six months older.
- Jose Pina was actually Onely Perez and two years, two months older.
- Francisco Selmo was actually Martin Selmo and four years older.

- Carlos Valdes was actually Roberto Perez and four years, five months older.
- Isabel Gibron was actually Julio Gibron and four years, six months older.

Isabel? Yup, that's a girl's name. Julio Gibron passed himself off as his younger sister and twenty-four years of age when he was traded to the Padres in 1999. Instead, he was nearly twenty-nine years old. Isabel—I mean Julio—Gibron was given his pink slip after the subterfuge came to light. She/he was not alone. According to an internal audit by Major League Baseball, 550 players had falsified their names or their birth dates, including Deivi Cruz, the Padres starting shortstop in 2002. Cruz aged overnight when a document check revealed that he was twenty-nine years old, not twenty-six years old.

Three years is a big difference, and that's why players try to shave years off their resume. A younger player has a greater chance of catching on with a team, and once he's earned a roster spot, a greater chance of being paid *mucho* bucks. A seventeen-year-old prospect who demonstrates power, speed, and fielding ability will sign a far larger contract than a twenty-one-year-old. That's the way baseball has always operated. Players with more years left in their short career will always be worth more to the general manager signing the checks.

The age-old phenomenon is not limited to foreign players. I've asked white players how old they were, only to hear the reply, "You mean my baseball age?" But they said it with a wink and a nod, and no one ever got away with it for long. Not so in the baseball-crazy countries in the Caribbean, where lying about your age has become an art form. In Third World countries where the per capita income is $1,500 a year, those able to run, hit, and throw at the highest levels will earn untold riches if they're good enough to make the major leagues. They, in turn, will be able to support their loved ones back home.

So some Latin players lie about their age. *Buscones*—the independent scouts who beat the bushes in the hinterlands—encourage young, talented players to fudge their age, adopt a younger brother's

identity, or alter their birth certificate. This practice, practically insti-
tutionalized, had been going on for years, and it's likely that no one
would have been the wiser until the INS told Major League Baseball that players caught falsifying their identity would never qualify
for a visa to enter the United States. That caused ball clubs like the
Padres to perform an internal audit of official documents, and like
cockroaches running for darkness after the bedroom light has been
turned on, several hundred players were caught red-handed.

I don't pretend to understand how desperate these foreign
prospects are to sign with a Major League team, but what I can
understand is that God does not want us to lie, and that trumps
everything. If you tell a few untruths, you will reap a harvest of dishonesty, fraud, and corrupt behavior.

I realize that most Americans probably shrug their shoulders and
don't really care that players like Deivi Cruz passed himself off as three
years younger. If so, I have two words for you: Danny Altamonte.

Remember him? He was the Little League pitcher who single-
handedly pitched the Rolando Paulino All-Stars—a collection of players from the Bronx—to the U.S. championship game at the 2001
Little League World Series in Williamsport, Pennsylvania. Believe me,
every Little League player dreams of one day getting to Williamsport,
where ESPN and ABC Sports televise the playoffs nationwide.

I remember watching young Danny and his lanky leg kick blow
fastballs by four-foot, eleven-inch players whose knees were knocking
as they struggled to conquer their fear about staying in the batter's box
against him. The announcers said that the speed gun clocked Danny
pitching faster than seventy miles per hour. Seventy miles per hour
from a mound just forty-six feet away from the plate translates to
ninety-two-mile-per-hour heat. That's major league stuff! No wonder
the scared batters were stepping into the bucket and bailing out.

It didn't help that Danny, who stood five feet, eight inches tall,
towered over batters, which earned him the nickname "The Little
Unit"—a play off Randy Johnson ("The Big Unit") and the blazing

speed he generates with his six-foot, ten-inch height. The way Danny overpowered defenseless batters with a mature array of fastballs, change-ups, and curves was amazing to watch; he appeared to be a young man playing with mere boys. In one game at Williamsport, Altamonte pitched a perfect game, whiffing the first fifteen batters to face him. No one could lay a bat against him.

Under the glare of the national spotlight, Danny was a hero—the second coming of Randy Johnson. Ken Griffey Jr. called him to wish him good luck. He was interviewed on national TV, although he needed an interpreter to translate his Spanish. The media marveled at how he struck out sixty-two of the seventy-two batters he faced and allowed just three hits in four games.

An enterprising reporter with *Sports Illustrated* began doing some background checking. It seems that a year earlier, in March 2000, Danny had moved to New York City from the Dominican Republic. An examination of birth ledgers in the civil records building in his hometown revealed that Danny was born in 1987, not 1989, making him fourteen years old.

Listen, two years is a huge difference between the ages of twelve and fourteen. Those are the puberty years, the period when boys go from being apple-cheeked kids with peach fuzz to maturing young men sprouting pimples and facial hair. Testosterone kicks into overdrive, and muscles and sinew develop as never before.

The evidence was irrefutable against Danny. Little League officials called the news "disheartening." Danny's team had to forfeit all their games, and youth baseball came under a dark cloud.

What a sad, sad story. It later turned out that Danny was in this country illegally, and the reason he didn't know any English was because his father and stepmother, who provided a home for him in the Bronx, never enrolled him in school. I guess he was brought to the States to work on his two-seam fastball, not his three R's.

"We had to commit this little fraud to give this opportunity to our child," said Inoa Sanchez, the boy's stepmother.

No, you didn't have to commit a "little" fraud, Mrs. Sanchez. Danny could have played in a Babe Ruth youth baseball program against players his own age. But you and your husband didn't want a level playing field.

Fifteen Minutes of Fame

One reason why parents willingly have their fourteen-year-old son play against twelve-year-olds is just so they can get on camera. It used to be that ABC showed the final game of the Little League World Series on its *Wide World of Sports* show during the dog days of August.

No longer. A week of round-robin play is now an ESPN staple, and it's possible that several teams will get on national TV several times before the final game. Team managers who were running a True Value store back home are miked up and are expected to coach like Joe Torre or Tommy Lasorda while America listens to their every word. Young players whose voices are still cracking are interviewed after the game and asked what kind of pitch they hit. Highlights are looped on *SportsCenter*.

This has to be heady stuff for youngsters who have never faced the media's bright glare. I think hearing Chris Berman say his rapid-fire "back-back-back-back" as my home-run ball went over the fence would have given me a big head at that age.

Just as today's younger players imitate the wheelhouse swings of Barry Bonds, they also imitate some of their over-the-top behavior. Some try to be cool and do the forearm bash, just as Mark McGwire did. Others are more demonstrative and strut their stuff by pointing to themselves after hitting a double. A couple of years ago, a young player from Harlem stood outside the batter's box, pointed to the outfield with his bat, and then doubled off the center field fence. Call it a junior version of Babe's called shot.

I guess this is a situation where life imitates art—what players see major league players doing on TV. I think it would be better if our twelve-year-olds acted like twelve-year-olds, not like major leaguers acting like twelve-year-olds.

They Said It

"All the Padres need is a fly ball in the air."

—Jerry Coleman, San Diego Padre radio announcer

MAY I TAKE YOUR ORDER?   22

When I was playing for the San Diego Padres in the early 1980s, we took a lot of ribbing around the league for our uniforms. Brown must have been in back in those days—I guess as a nod to the Juniperro Serra and the brown-robed Franciscan friars, who founded San Diego in 1769. The Padres inaugural season in 1969 was exactly two hundred years after the first California mission was founded not far from San Diego Bay.

When I came along in 1982, the Padres played in brown caps with mustard-yellow trim and white home uniforms accented in brown and the same garish yellow. Yellow sanitary hose with brown leggings completed the fashion statement. I can assure you that no one was clamoring to come play in Padre brown and yellow. First baseman Steve Garvey said he felt like a taco when he took the field. The players joked that they didn't know whether they would be asked for their autograph or a quarter-pounder with cheese. Our uniforms were so *ug-lee* that ESPN ranked ours fourth on its end-of-the-twentieth-century list of the worst uniforms in the past hundred years.

The only baseball team to beat us on ESPN's list was the Chicago White Sox in the early 1980s. Sox owner Bill Veeck dressed his club back in softball uniforms—black shirts (not tucked in) with white collars and white pants that ended at the knee. (Let's blame that on the disco craze.)

That's embarrassing—playing baseball in short pants. Not that we didn't have other clubs whose uniforms got smacked with an ugly stick. Remember those orange-and-yellow jerseys that Nolan Ryan used to pitch in when he was with the Houston Astros? Owner Charley Finley dressed his Oakland A's in canary-yellow from cap to stocking—with white cleats.

The funny thing about this is that some of these old, ugly uniforms are actually cool these days. In fact, we're finding out that people are quite willing to pay lots of money for "classic" uniforms from the past. A replica of Nolan Ryan's 1980s Houston Astros uniform, splashed with bright orange and yellow, retails for $300 and up in stores like Men's Land in malls around the country. Other sports are retro as well: You can also buy everything from a replica of Jim Brown's No. 32 jersey from the 1964 Cleveland Browns to early MJ jerseys from the Chicago Bulls.

Why are throwback jerseys commanding such big money? Very old has become very cool again because hip-hop artists prance around in their music videos wearing the retro gear. Then pop culture athletes like Kobe Bryant and Shaquille O'Neal wear different throwback jerseys during road trips. It's a fad that will run its course, but for now, they are the got-to-have accessories when you're chillin' with your friends.

I should take some of my old uniforms out of mothballs and put them up on eBay. But there's one uniform that I would like to add to my collection. A couple of seasons ago, the Pads unveiled "cammo" jerseys—uniforms with camouflage tops that looked like something you'd pick up at the Camp Pendleton PX. I think they're cool looking and would be the perfect fashion accessory on my next hunting trip.

I think I want one of those camouflage uniforms. I have just one request: Will the Padres put "Dravecky" and my old number—43—on the back?

A Way to Lose Your Uniform

A lesson in the way not to start a major league career. Ron Wright was called up by the Seattle Mariners as a designated hitter. In his first three at bats, Wright struck out, hit into a double play, and then hit into a rare triple play. The snakebit rookie was shipped back to the minors the next day.

They Said It

"He lakes a blutt."

—Ron Fairly, Seattle Mariners radio announcer

CHASING MY DREAMS

I was just out of high school when Dad said, "Let's go see the Indians play."

Dad didn't have to ask twice. Although I was a National League fan, I had a special place in my heart for the Cleveland Indians since they played only seventy-five miles from my hometown of Boardman, Ohio.

On the drive to the ballpark, Dad and I learned that a rookie named Dennis Eckersley would be on the mound that day for the Indians.

"Can we watch him warm up?" I asked Dad. As a young pitcher for Youngstown State University who carried aspirations to make it someday to the big leagues, I liked studying pitchers as they went about their craft—how they warmed up, how they started batters off, how they pitched themselves out of jams, and how they fielded their position.

Dad and I found a spot right above the Indian bullpen, and we had a great view of Eckersley heating up that afternoon. After a dozen or so warm-up tosses, Dennis really began throwing very hard. I mean, he was bringing it.

"So, do you think you can throw that hard?" Dad asked.

"Yeah, sure I do," I replied with the confidence that only a nineteen-year-old can deliver.

"Do you think you'll be able to do something like that someday?"

That was the first time Dad had ever asked me about my dream. "Yeah, sure I do, Dad. I really want to pitch in the major leagues."

Dad didn't laugh or tell me not to be so ridiculous or suggest that I didn't have a chance. Instead, he encouraged me just as any father should. "Just remember two things," he said that day. "Whatever you choose to do, work hard at it. Don't shortchange yourself, be the best you can be. But more important, go out and have fun."

Those were words of great advice. As I got serious about my faith when I became a Christian a few years later, I knew that being everything that God wanted me to be as a person would demand hard work on my part. If I tried to shortchange my walk with Christ, I had a Coach who would know that I was putting in a weak effort to improve myself spiritually.

I put in the effort, and I've tried to have fun. Sure, I've experienced some deep valleys, but the highs have been better than the lows. I'm glad Dad told me to enjoy myself, because I have. I cut up in the clubhouse just like the rest of the guys. I hope I showed some of my teammates that Christians can enjoy life as much as if not more than others, that Christianity is more than a bunch of thee's and thou's and "don't do that." It's a lifelong relationship with Christ, and I'm glad it's been part of my life for twenty years now.

Colorful Eck Spressions

I have to say more about Dennis Eckersley, who was an American League guy when I was playing. He had an incredibly colorful way of talking about baseball that became famous around both leagues. "The Eck," as he was called, spoke a language that needed a United Nations translator. You had to be hip to the latest Eckspeak emitting from his lips.

Eck said that pitchers who threw fast delivered "cheese" to the plate, unless the catcher signaled for a "yakker," or curveball. An inside pitch was in the batter's "kitchen," but a fast pitch over the heart of the plate was said to be "salad" for the hitter. A head-hunting throw that caused a batter to duck prompted a move known as a "kudo."

Thus, if you could throw high-ninety mph "cheese" and a big "yakker," you could ask for a lot of "iron"—money.

"Pitching is simple," the Eck said one day. "Cheese for the kitchen and a yakker for the kudo."

CALLED UP

Say what?

Anyone who can keep up with jargon like that deserves a lot of iron, but colorful speech and off-the-wall phrases have been part of baseball since the dead ball era. The game of baseball, according to author Paul Dickson *(The Dickson Baseball Dictionary)*, coins words, phrases, nicknames, and expressions faster than Barry Bonds launching another round-tripper into McCovey's Cove. In his exhaustive volume on baseball nomenclature, Dickson compiled more than seven thousand terms relating to the Grand Old Game.

A "can of corn" is a high, lazy fly ball to the outfield. A ball that bounces off the plate is called a "Baltimore chop." Line drives are "frozen ropes," but soft flies that fall in front of the charging outfielders—which used to be known as "Texas Leaguers" or "dying quails"—are now called a "Can't Teach That," since, presumably, you can't teach a young batter to poke the ball between the infield and the outfield.

I love baseball slang. I'm going to give you a little test. Match the following terms with the definitions:

1. Gettysburg Address	A. a home run
2. chin music	B. a batted ball that comes right to a defensive player
3. a snow cone	
4. a deuce	C. a control pitcher who paints the black
5. a Picasso	
6. a tater	D. a ruckus with the umpires
7. a rhubarb	E. a term describing all the gossip that takes place about baseball during the winter months
8. hot stove league	
9. room service	
10. an iron glove	
	F. a grand-slam home run
	G. somebody who can't field
	H. a high and tight pitch inside

I. a catch made at the very end of the glove
J. a curveball signaled by the catcher

2.H	4.J	6.A	8.E	10.G
1.F	3.I	5.C	7.D	9.B

Answer key:

Results:

- All ten correct: You know your baseball! I want you coaching third base on the Dave Dravecky All-Stars.
- 7–8 correct: You've got great stuff, but you need a little more seasoning before you're ready for The Show.
- 5–6 correct: You're stuck in Triple A.
- 3–4: You got shelled. Time to head for the showers.
- 0–2: Back to the bush leagues for you.

Many churchgoers probably don't realize this, but we often use Christian "slang" and utter certain expressions that sound like a foreign tongue to those who haven't been around church very much.

It's called "Christianese," and we have to be careful what we say when we're around the "unchurched"—oops, I mean non-Christians. Our little sayings often come off sounding holier-than-thou or even off-putting to those who haven't darkened many church doors in their lives. I'm talking about phrases like:

- "I'll be praying for you during my quiet time."
- "Would you mind if I shared your prayer need with my accountability group?"
- "So, how's your walk with the Lord going?"

- "I really need to get back into the Word these days."
- "My personal time has been especially sweet with the Lord."
- "Last night, while I was praying in the Spirit. . . ."

Huh?

That's what your non-Christians friends will be thinking. You see, speaking in jargon—whether it's Christianese or the latest slang from the dugout—means you're part of a club. Those who aren't up to speed or can't follow along feel excluded. First Corinthians 2:14 says, "But people who aren't Christians can't understand these truths from God's Spirit. It all sounds foolish to them because only those who have the Spirit can understand what the Spirit means" (NLT).

That's why we have to be so careful in how we speak when we're around people who don't know Christ. The apostle Paul said, "Be wise in all your contacts with them," referring to those who don't know about salvation through Jesus Christ. "Let your conversation be gracious as well as sensible, for then you will have the right answer for everyone" (Colossians 4:5–6, TLB).

And people are looking for answers these days.

They Said It

"Last night, I neglected to mention something that bears repeating."

—Ron Fairly, Seattle Mariners radio announcer

Maybe it's because we have plenty of time on our hands, sitting on the bench and watching pitchers and batters scratch and spit so much, but we've sure come up with plenty of synonyms for the plain old vanilla curveball. Try these on for size:

- breaking ball
- bender
- slider
- number two (since the catcher usually flashes two fingers signaling for a curveball)
- the deuce
- the hook
- Hook Johnson
- Captain Hook
- Uncle Charlie
- Lord Charles
- The Local
- yellow hammer
- yakker (courtesy of Dennis Eckersley)
- the yack attack
- the rainbow
- the outdrop
- slide piece
- snake
- spinner

Sometimes "deuces" don't curve, which makes them a sitting target. Curves that don't curve end up as:

- a round-tripper
- a circuit clout
- a big fly
- a salami
- a moonshot
- a tater
- going yard
- a big tomato
- a blast, bomb, dinger, slam, wallop, shot, jolt, cookie, donk, poke, bonk, bolt, cork, and rocket (as in launched)

So the next time you want to impress friends with a "home-run call" just like the announcers do on TV or radio, go with one of these:

- "Elvis has left the building!"
- "Light the cannons, boys!"
- "That's so far out, it's RuPaul!"
- "Get your rye bread out, Grandma, because it's grand salami time!"
- "Whip up some gravy because that baby's smashed!"
- "I hope a flight attendant is booked on that flight!"
- "The National Weather Service has just issued a home-run watch!"
- "Open a window, Aunt Nellie, because here it comes!"

Again, I ask the question: What sport has more colorful expressions than baseball?

They Said It

"From the way Denny's shaking his head, he's either got an injured shoulder or a gnat in his eye."

—Jerry Coleman, San Diego Padre radio announcer

THE WIT AND WISDOM OF YOGI BERRA

25

He's been called the father of the faux pas, the master of the malaprop. After all these years of saying something funny or farcical without batting an eye, Yogi Berra is starting to receive his due.

Roger Williams University in Bristol, Rhode Island, presented Yogi with an honorary doctorate at a recent commencement. I guess we can call him Dr. Berra now, a man of letters and refinement.

Not bad for a guy with an eighth-grade education.

Yogi, who's now in his late seventies, is a Hall of Fame catcher who played for the New York Yankees when they ruled the baseball universe from the late 1940s to the early 1960s. He had this knack for saying the most head-scratching stuff like, "I'm wearing these gloves for my hands." Well, sure you are, Yogi.

When you stop and think about it—and that's what you usually have to do after you hear or read another Yogism—Yogi is usually right. The neat thing is that you can unpack great spiritual truths from Yogi's classic sayings. Let's take a look at a few, followed by my commentary on how this could apply to our spiritual lives:

- **"You've got to be very careful if you don't know where you're going, because you might not get there."**

  I mentioned this quotation in my introduction, but so many people go through life aimlessly, not looking past tomorrow. "A life not evaluated is not worth living," the Greek philosopher Socrates said one time. If you don't know where you're going in life, you *won't* get there. It's like the time someone said to Yogi, "Hey, I think we're lost." Yogi replied, "Yeah, but we're making great time."

- **"If you can't imitate him, don't copy him."**

  If you flip this around, Yogi could be saying, "If you can imitate Christ, do copy him."

- **"Always go to other people's funerals, otherwise they won't come to yours."**

  This is another way of stating the Golden Rule, right? Do unto others as you would have others do unto you.

- **"Include me out."**

  We are in this world, but we should not be of the world. Romans 12:2 tells us, "And do not be conformed to this world, but be transformed by the renewing of your mind, so that you may prove what the will of God is, that which is good and acceptable and perfect" (NASB).

- **"A nickel ain't worth a dime any more."**

  Everything on earth is temporal and won't last. Jesus said, "Heaven and earth will pass away, but my words will never pass away." This statement is so important that it's repeated word for word in Matthew, Mark, and Luke.

- **"The other teams could make trouble for us if they win."**

  Yup, and Satan could make trouble for us if we let him win.

- **"We were overwhelming underdogs."**

  That's right, and that's what we were like before we knew Christ: we were overwhelmed, and we were definitely underdogs.

- **"If the people don't want to come out to the park, nobody's gonna stop them."**

If people don't want to go to church, nobody's going to stop them either. Our churches must be relevant to today's culture.

- **"Because it gets late early."** (Yogi said this after being asked on why it's so tough to play left field on day games at Yankee Stadium.)

  Many people are unaware that it's getting late early for them, or that they may soon die and face judgment before the Lord Jesus. Life has a way of getting late earlier than you think.

- **"You can observe a lot by just watching."**

  You sure can. Our non-Christian friends and acquaintances at work are watching us continually, observing how we react when tragedy hits or our choice of words in the lunchroom.

- **"Slump? I ain't in no slump. I just ain't hittin'."**

  Isn't that just like the human condition? We are in continual denial when we go through life without God. We need Christ.

- **"This is like déjà vu all over again."**

  Ecclesiastes 1:9 reminds us that there is nothing new under the sun. We keep making the same mistakes as history repeats itself.

- **"In baseball, you don't know nothin'."**

  And our ways are not God's ways, says Isaiah 55:8–9, which means that we don't know nothin' when it comes to the mind of God.

- **"It ain't over till it's over."**

  Our lives are a continual marathon, so we must endure until the end of our days, knowing that we can do anything through Christ who strengthens us (Philippians 4:13).

- **"If the world was perfect, it wouldn't be."**

Yogi has it dead-on here. At times, we may think things are perfect, and we may harbor these pie-in-the-sky dreams of what the world would be like if everything was perfect, but our world is never going to look that way. It can't. Only Christ is perfect.

- **"The future ain't what it used to be."**
  For those of us who have personal relationships with Christ, the future ain't what it used to be. We had *no* future before we knew him; now we have the greatest possible future ahead of us—eternal life with Christ.

Déjà Vu All Over Again

It was fun to consider how the wit and wisdom of Yogi Berra relates to our faith. Now let's sit back and enjoy some more examples from the fertile mind of this true American legend. Thanks, Yogi, for being so transparent.

"I'd find the fellow who lost it, and if he was poor, I'd return it."

—Yogi, answering Casey Stengel's question,
"What would you do if you found a million dollars?"

"I don't know. I'm not in shape yet."

—Yogi, when asked his cap size

"Baseball is 90 percent mental. The other half is physical."

"How can you think and hit at the same time?"

"Gee, Joey, that's the earliest I've ever been late."

—Yogi, after arriving fifteen minutes after
a scheduled 4 p.m. appointment

"When you come to a fork in the road, take it."

THE WIT AND WISDOM OF YOGI BERRA

"You better cut that pizza into four pieces because I'm not hungry enough to eat six."

"He must have made that before he died."

> —Yogi, after seeing a Steve McQueen movie

"What's wrong with dem kids now?"

> —Yogi, after learning that his wife, Carmen, had taken the children to see the movie *Dr. Zhivago*

"No one goes there any more—it's too crowded."

> —Yogi, referring to a popular restaurant named Charlie's

"I knew I was going to take the wrong train, so I left early."

"It's pretty far, but it doesn't seem like it."

"It was impossible to get a conversation going because everybody was talking too much."

Interviewer: "Why, you're a fatalist!"
Yogi: "You mean I save postage stamps? Not me."

Teammate: "Yogi, what time is it?"
Yogi: "You mean right now?"

They Said It

"The similarities between me and my father are different."

—Dale Berra, talking about his father, Yogi

OUT FOR A WALK

26

The most exasperating thing a pitcher can do is to walk the batter with the bases loaded. The *second* most exasperating way to drive your manager crazy is to walk a batter to start the inning. Whenever I issued a free pass to the first batter of the inning, I felt this sense of foreboding on the pitcher's mound. I saw looks of concern from the dugout. Everyone was worried that something bad would happen.

My coaches and teammates had reasons to chew those sunflower seeds a little faster. They knew baseball, and when you start off the inning with a walk, the potential for mischief is there, especially late in the game with a tie score. Now you're pitching out of the stretch, worried about keeping the runner close to the bag. Fortunately, I was a lefty, which meant I was looking straight at the runner and the first baseman as I held my stretch, but I was still not pitching out of a full windup with my full concentration directed at just the batter. Now I had a runner to worry about.

This was a time to pitch well and pitch carefully. A single usually put runners on the corners, a double to the alley could score a runner from first base, and a pitch in a batter's wheelhouse could make a nice souvenir for a fan in the bleachers.

You have to know when to hold 'em and when to fold 'em because there are times when it's better to walk a batter than to give him something to hit. You may have a runner on second base, first base open, less than two outs, and a slow runner in the on-deck circle. That's the time to walk a good hitter so that you can work for the double-play ball.

If I was facing the number-three or number-four hitter in that situation—man on second, less than two outs—I usually pitched around him, unless the manager ordered me to issue him an intentional walk.

I had a better chance getting out the fifth or sixth hitter in the lineup in that situation.

Pitchers have just as much pride as anyone else, and sometimes they *want* to face the other team's best hitter in a pressure-packed situation. That was the case when Goose Gossage, the best closer I ever saw, faced Kirk Gibson, the Detroit Tigers' No. 3 hitter, in the 1984 World Series. This Padres-Tigers matchup was called the "Fast Food Series" because it pitted McDonald's verses Domino's—Joan Kroc (whoes husband Ray, the founder of McDonald's, died just before the 1984 season started) owned the Padres, and Tom Monaghan, the founder of Domino's Pizza, owned the Tigers.

Here was the situation. The Padres were playing before a partisan Tiger crowd at Tiger Stadium, down 3–1 in the series. There was no tomorrow, as they say. If we could win, however, then we'd have to fly back to San Diego for Game 6. Maybe some home cooking would help us pull off a miracle as we did against the Chicago Cubs in the National League Championship Series, when we fell behind 2–0 in a best-of-five before sweeping three in San Diego.

First order of business was winning Game 5. Kirk Gibson's two-run shot in the first inning put us behind, but we battled back to tie the score in the fourth, 3–3. Then Gibson singled in the fifth and worked his way to third base. Batter Rusty Kuntz lifted a pop fly to right field that shouldn't have been deep enough to score Gibson. But right fielder Tony Gwynn lost the ball in the gray sky and yelled for second baseman Alan Wiggins to make the catch, who was backpedaling all the way. Gibson alertly tagged up and broke for the plate, beating a weak throw from Wiggins.

Goose Gossage, our feared reliever, was brought in with one out in the seventh to face Lance Parrish. The hometown fans chanted "Goose-buster"—a play off a popular Bill Murray movie of the day called *Ghostbusters*. Goose always liked road games and boisterous

119

crowds, but he got a fastball up against Parrish and watched him deposit it into the left field stands.

Parrish's homer made the score 5–3 for Detroit, but we didn't give up. Kurt Bevacqua homered in the top of the eighth to make it 5–4, which lifted our spirits in the bullpen, where I was hoping the phone would ring and tell me to start heating up. The feeling on our bench was that if Goose could hold them in their half of the eighth inning, then Destiny would ride with us during another ninth-inning rally. We had been playing like that all season, so there was no reason to expect that our rally caps wouldn't work again.

Then Detroit put men on second and third against Gossage. One out, first base open, and Kirk Gibson steps into the batter's box. From the Tiger dugout, Tiger manager Sparky Anderson flashed four fingers at Gibson, warning him that he would get intentionally walked. A free pass made sense: Gibson had been killing us all series and had already hit a home run and scored another run that day with a heads-up play.

But Kirk knew something about Goose Gossage, a bear of a competitor whose loosy-goosy windup, Fu Manchu moustache, and 98-mph fastball made him one tough hombre when the game was on the line. Kirk flashed five fingers twice at Sparky Anderson, indicating that he wanted to bet ten dollars that Gossage *would* pitch to him. Sparky nodded his assent to the bet.

Time out! When it became apparent that Gossage wanted to pitch to Gibson, our manager, Dick Williams, sprinted out to the mound for a conference with Gossage and the Padre infield.

"Let me pitch to Gibson," said Gossage. "I've had good success against him in the past."

That was not what Williams wanted to hear. With the World Series on the line, the prudent route was to walk Gibson and play for the double-play ball. But Gossage was breathing fire. "I can get him out," he said, so Williams relented, and Gibson collected on his ten dollar bet.

Gibson also collected his second home run of the game when he smashed Goose's offering a long, long way. His towering home run to right field put the Tigers out in front 8–4, and that was all she wrote for the 1984 World Series.

Sometimes we want to do things our way when the situation calls for caution. Sometimes we don't want to listen to someone who knows better.

That someone in our lives—Jesus Christ—has been through everything we face. The next time you feel the Lord is whispering "Careful" in your ear, don't insist on having it your way.

Just do what he says and keep pitching your best.

Don't Look Up

Let me tell another story about the 1984 World Series. This involves one of the leading characters on the team—Kurt Bevacqua, a thirty-seven-year-old player for whom the word "journeyman" was invented, said one *Sports Illustrated* sportswriter. He had played in the majors for thirteen years, but when you added up the games he played and the at bats, it amounted to four years of service. He was no gazelle on the base paths, was average with the glove, and couldn't hit for power. A role player.

So when Kurt, playing before a home crowd on the world's biggest stage, hit a three-run homer in Game 2 to give us our first lead, he went bananas. As he rounded first base, he pirouetted like Barishnikov before trotting toward second base and third base with his index finger high in the air. After rounding third in the bedlam of San Diego Jack Murphy Stadium, he blew a two-handed kiss to his wife, Carrie, sitting in the players' wives section behind first base. His teammates nearly gang-tackled him. I would have been there if I hadn't been out in the left field bullpen.

I was happy for Kurt. He waited a long time for this special moment. We used to tease him in the clubhouse because Kurt's biggest claim to fame prior to the 1984 World Series was when he won the

1975 big league bubble-gum-blowing contest. On another occasion, he caught baseballs dropped from a twenty-five-story skyscraper in downtown San Diego.

Pitch to Kirk Gibson with the World Series on the line? Yeah, I'd do that, if the skipper brought me in. But catch a ball dropped 250 feet above me?

No way!

They Said It

"Raise the urinals."

—Darrel Chaney, on how management could keep the Atlanta Braves on their toes

TAKE YOUR BASE, SON   27

A walk is as good as a hit.

How often did you hear your Little League coach remind you that from the dugout as you waited to hit a 3–1 pitch?

There isn't much glory in accepting a base on balls and trotting to first base—although Pete Rose used to charge first base after receiving a walk (which is why they called him "Charlie Hustle"). They don't hold parades for guys who break the all-time base-on-balls record.

When Rickey Henderson accepted his record-setting 2,063[d] walk as a Padre, breaking Babe Ruth's career record, it was a one-night story on ESPN *SportsCenter*. Contrast that to the media circus surrounding Mark McGwire as he took dead aim at Roger Maris's home-run record, the anticipation building up to Hank Aaron's 715th home run, or the hoopla accorded to Pete Rose when he slapped a single for his 4,192[nd] hit. I was there in Cincinnati when Rose passed Ty Cobb as the all-time hit leader, and believe me, it was a big deal. They stopped the game for ten minutes so that Pete could take a bow, hug his family, and say a few words.

Contrast the hitting records to the lowly walk. The perception among some fans is that batters who look for walks are role players taking the path of least resistance. But as a pitcher, I held a different view. I *hated* giving up walks because more often than not, that runner on first base had a way of coming all the way home.

Let me expand on this point. Steve Garvey, my first baseman when I played for the Padres, didn't like to leave his bat on the shoulder when he stepped into the batter box. He viewed himself as an aggressive hitter, someone who "took his cuts" when the pitch was made. Consequently, Steve didn't walk much, averaging just 29.5 walks per year. The Garv also never scored more than a hundred runs in a season.

Contrast this to Barry Bonds, who has this larger-than-life image at the plate—a one-man wrecking crew who smashes home runs at will. But many fans overlook the fact that Barry has a discerning eye at the plate, much like a gourmand who appraises food presentation at a culinary show. Barry is willing to overlook pitches that he doesn't like, and those attributes make him especially dangerous as a hitter. During the 2001 season, when Barry set the all-time home-run mark of 73, he also broke Babe Ruth's single-season walk record with 177 walks, seven more than the Bambino. Barry scored a career-high 129 runs in 2001, good for third in the National League.

After he set the single-season home-run record, pitchers afforded Barry a higher level of respect the following season. He shattered his base-on-balls record in 2002 with 198 walks and was third in the league again with 117 runs scored. But don't forget that Barry hit twenty-seven fewer home runs, which count as a run scored. Though the Giant outfielder knew he was being pitched around, he proved his patience. Barry was willing to wait until he got a pitch to hit. His deliberate manner translated into the league's highest batting average at .370. Who would have thought that a home-run hitter could also hit for average in this day and age? He followed that up by hitting .341 in 2003, hitting forty-five home runs in just 130 games.

I don't think I would have pitched around Barry (unless ordered to do so by the manager) because I understand how walks kill you as a pitcher. Not only did you have to contend with base runners, but you knew you were guaranteed to deliver *more* pitches, and a tiring pitcher tends to get his pitches up. Pitches up in the strike zone tend to land in the upper deck. That's why I would have had my game face on if I had ever been handed the ball against Ted Williams. He was famous for knowing the strike zone down to the last square inch, and if my pitch were one inch off the plate, he'd let it pass by as if my stuff wasn't worthy of his attention.

Ted's walks and .344 career batting average translated into a ridiculous career on-base percentage of .482. Each time Ted waltzed toward first base, however, his critics charged that if Williams expanded his strike zone, he would help out his team more. They pointed to his rival Joe DiMaggio, who didn't walk often, saying that the Yankee Clipper's assertive batting style won pennants. But Joe D played on a better team.

Taking a walk is like starting our long spiritual walk. Often times, the payoff is years—often decades, sometimes a whole lifetime—away. The temptation is to swing at a pitch just outside the strike zone, just as we're tempted to grab at something just outside the "strike zone" of godly behavior. Sneaking a peek at Internet porn. Making an improper pass at a woman just to see how she'd respond. Padding the expense report.

It's better to let those temptations pass by and take your base. Sure, it's longer to reach home, and the world doesn't stand up and applaud when you are walked, but you're on the path that God wants you to be. Remember, you have Christ batting behind you in the order. He will bring you around the horn and back home—your eternal home with him.

They Said It

"If a man can beat you, walk him."

—Satchel Paige, ageless pitching wonder

BREAKING DOWN WALLS 28

Do you want to know what is the most exciting play in baseball—for the fans *and* for the pitcher, whose heart in his throat?

It's a deep fly ball into one of the power alleys that can just clear the fence or stay in the ballpark. Can the center fielder giving chase get there in time to make the leaping, acrobatic catch?

Outfielders who can leap above the fence and rob the batter of a home run are guaranteed a spot on *Baseball Tonight*. Slow-motion replays are often the subject of watercooler talk at work. Major league ballpark designers have done a smart thing in recent years by putting in eight-foot-tall padded "fences" ringing the outfield. Eight feet is just the right height for an outfielder to leap up, snatch a ball that's broken the plane into home-run territory, and fall back to the warning track with the baseball in his mitt.

Torii Hunter is the leading practitioner of this art. The Minnesota Twins outfielder has been making above-the-wall grabs since he broke in with the Twins in 1997. It helps that the Metrodome has one of the lowest fences at seven feet, but that still does not diminish Torii's skill at turning home-run balls into long outs.

Torii made a big splash at the 2002 All-Star Game when Barry Bonds lashed a fastball deep into center field. Torii sprinted to the back wall, waited . . . waited . . . and then timed his jump perfectly to catch the ball well above the fence. "Taking a home run away from someone is definitely better than hitting one myself," Torii said.

The Twins center fielder doesn't mind throwing his body at a padded wall if a play can be made. In the minor leagues, however, where fence padding is a hit or miss venture, Torii once ran for a well-hit ball and didn't stop running until he charged through a plywood fence. It's a play that pops up in all those crazy "baseball blooper" videos, and maybe you've seen the footage of Torii running full-speed-ahead into a plywood wall only to have it disintegrate into pieces. It's hilarious, although Torii was pretty woozy afterward.

These days, Torii picks his spots. The only stadiums where he *won't* crash into the wall are Safeco Field in Seattle and Fenway Park in Boston, where padding is nonexistent, but in every other stadium, he says that he's willing to crash into outfield walls because "I have to do it for my pitchers."

That's music to the ears of any pitcher, man.

They Said It

"The better he gets, the better he's going to be."

—Kirby Puckett, the Twins Hall of Fame outfielder, when asked
about center fielder Torii Hunter.

SIGN ME UP   29

After my All-Star season in 1983, my contract was up. The Padres
wanted me in their plans for the future, so they offered what I
thought was a generous three-year contract calling for $150,000 in
1984, $240,000 in 1985, and $360,000 in 1986. That would be
$750,000 to play baseball for three years, which looked like all the
money in the world to Jan and me. We hadn't forgotten that I was
two years removed from earning a few hundred bucks a month in
Double A ball.

I know—these figures look like chump change compared to
what the players pull down today. Did you know that the major
league *minimum* is $300,000 today, and the average salary for start-
ing pitchers is $3,300,000 per season? That's a lot of zeros! When I
played my last game in 1989, the average baseball salary was
$512,804. During the 2003 season, that figure had jumped nearly
500 percent in less than fifteen years to $2,555,476.

I know. That sounds like Monopoly money, and today's players don't know how good they have it. Not me. When I received that $750,000 contract tender from the Padres, my knee-jerk reaction was to say, "Where's the bottom line? I want to sign."

Some players thought I should hold out for more—not for my benefit, but for theirs! They said that if I signed that contract, then it could impact what they could extract from the owners during contract negotiations.

I listened to their concerns, and if I felt I was being totally low-balled, I wouldn't have signed the three-year deal. I thought what the Padres were offering was fair in relation to what other young pitchers around the league were getting. Did I want to go through acrimonious haggling and put the Padres through the ringer for an extra $20,000 a year?

No, because the other players were not my priority—my family was my priority. I wanted to provide for Jan and my children, and I saw the Padre contract offer as an opportunity to provide some financial security for us. This particular three-year contract had 750,000 guarantees, if you asked me. And I was playing a game that I loved very much, so that was enough for me. I wasn't going to make money an issue.

I was too young to know that I was making a wise decision, but I've watched players sign these megabucks contracts over the years and then have to deal with the burden of expectations on their shoulders. When I joined the Padres in 1982, Ray Kroc was still smarting from the disastrous free-agent signing of Oscar Gamble, who had a career year with the Chicago White Sox in 1977 when he hit thirty-one home runs. Ray gave him $2.85 million over six years, but he lasted only one season in San Diego, hitting just seven home runs.

Still, as we players said in the clubhouse, no one ever put a gun to the heads of the owners for offering such outrageous sums of money to play a sandlot game. But what was Texas Ranger owner

Tom Hicks thinking when he agreed to pay Alex Rodriguez $252 million over ten seasons?

During the 2002 season, here was the Top Ten Salary list:

1. Alex Rodriguez of the Texas Rangers: $22,000,000
2. Carlos Delgado of the Toronto Blue Jays: $19,400,000
3. Kevin Brown of the Los Angeles Dodgers: $15,714,286
4. Manny Ramirez of the Boston Red Sox: $15,462,727
5. Barry Bonds of the San Francisco Giants: $15,000,000
6. Sammy Sosa of the Chicago Cubs: $15,000,000
7. Derek Jeter of the New York Yankees: $14,000,000
8. Pedro Martinez of the Boston Red Sox: $14,000,000
9. Shawn Green of the Los Angeles Dodgers: $13,416,667
10. Randy Johnson of the Arizona Diamondbacks: $13,350,000

This ranking hasn't changed much since 2002 because the owners are finally demonstrating some financial restraint. Yes, I know, we are talking incomprehensible amounts of money, but what is really incomprehensible is that Alex Rodriguez made more money than the entire Tampa Bay Devils Ray *team* in 2003. I would feel humbled if someone paid me $20,000,000 to pitch; it's so much money that I can't comprehend that amount.

But most of us Christians forget that Jesus Christ paid for our contracts and that he purchased us for a price— his blood. "For you know that it was not with perishable things such as silver or gold that you were redeemed from the empty way of life handed down to you from your forefathers, but with the precious blood of Christ, a lamb without blemish or defect," says 1 Peter 1:18–19.

It's easy to get caught up in the big dollars that today's ballplayers make, but we who know Christ have something worth infinitely more than an A-Rod $252 million contract. We have been given eternal life, purchased by someone who loved us so much that he willingly died on a cross so that we could have eternal life.

Investment Comeback

When I signed that fat contract with the Padres in 1983 for $750,000 over the next three years, I thought our money worries were over. I wouldn't say that we had money to burn, but compared to the few hundred bucks a month that I was getting in the minor leagues, a quarter of a million dollars per year—and up—looked like mighty tall cotton to me.

When ballplayers sit around and shoot the breeze, the subject of money is never far away. Perhaps that's because our salaries are a matter of public record and everyone knows what the other person is making. Or maybe it's because we're finally able to buy some of the nicer things in life, including a flashy wardrobe, tricked-up cars, and lavish homes.

The talk often turns to investments because if you make the right investments during your high-income years, you don't have to get a job selling shoes when your ball-playing days are over, as our predecessors did. You wouldn't believe how much locker-room talk centers around what's hot in the investment world and what's not.

"I've got this friend who's putting together a great deal. . . ."

How many times did I hear *that* in the locker room? So when I signed my first big contract, I suddenly had some money to "invest." I heard about this "great deal" all right—a chance to buy three condominiums in Arizona and two in California. It would be a great tax shelter, I was told, a rare opportunity to get in on the "ground floor."

This sounded too good to be true. What was a better investment than real estate? It wasn't as if I was blowing my money on gold chains or vacation homes in Hawaii. This was "piece of the rock" stuff.

I made two mistakes with this investment:

1. *When I talked to Jan about the investment, I didn't pay any attention to her advice.* I had this notion that since I was the head of the family, I should make all the financial decisions

when any counselor would tell me that Jan, who had an accounting background, had a better financial head on her shoulders.

2. *I failed to get wise counsel from others.* I heard an investment idea, and I ran with it. I ran because I was greedy.

Well, three seasons passed by, and my money was tied up in five condominiums. I had a little problem on my hands, too. I pitched with a sore elbow during the 1986 season and took a definite step backward in my career: I finished with an 9–11 record, my first losing record in the big leagues. The off-season also happened to be the year that the owners colluded together not to sign free agents. My agent felt a cool breeze coming from the Padre front office. So I sat . . . and I sat . . . and I wondered if my professional baseball career was over. Meanwhile, I wanted to unload five condominiums in a hurry.

But there was just one problem on that front: there was no market for condominium resales. In fact, I was "upside down," as they say in real estate, which meant that I owed more than they were worth

This time around, I sought the counsel of Jan and some wise friends who knew a lot more about real estate than I did. Proverbs 15:22 says, "Plans fail for lack of counsel, but with many advisers they succeed." Jan and I prayed together for our finances, but the situation was scary. We looked to each other for a way out of the mess I had gotten ourselves into.

We had to unload those five condos at fire-sale prices, which definitely took a large chunk of our net worth. Actually, we had to pay the buyer of the fifth and last condo $4,000 to make the deal happen. We also sold our San Diego dream house and moved into a smaller place. Meanwhile, the Padres tendered a one-year contract offer, but I had to make the team in spring training to collect on it.

I learned an important lesson about money that year, a lesson we put to good use two years later. Jan and I decided to move the family back to our hometown of Boardman, Ohio, and make that our permanent home. We bought a nice lot and directed an architect to begin designing a monster house with tons of square footage and all the bells and whistles—vaulted ceilings, granite countertops, and expensive fixtures.

Then Jan and I began talking. She remembered how nothing was certain in baseball—including those high-paying salaries. She had read a magazine article describing the importance of a modest lifestyle. "Do you think our house is modest?" she asked one evening.

"Uh, no," I said. "There's no way our dream house is modest."

After discussing it further, I knew what we had to do. I suggested that we cancel the architect, sell the lot, and find something cheaper. And that's what we did. Within a couple of months, we sold our lot, bought a smaller one, and picked out a home design from the developer. This became a house that we could like and we could afford.

Little did I know that in two years I would lose my career, my left arm, and my income (admittedly high) from playing baseball. But we had successfully downsized *before* all that happened, so we were able to live within our means in the years following the amputation.

You know, the Bible talks more about money than any other subject, and that's a good thing. Proverbs 21:20 tells us, "The wise man saves for the future, but the foolish man spends whatever he gets" (TLB).

I don't think I'm wise when it comes to money matters, but I know what foolish is. I hope you do, too.

They Said It

(Here's some investment advice)

"Rome wasn't born in a day."

—Johnny Logan, Milwaukee Braves shortstop

Some people say that baseball is no longer the national pastime, that football is America's top sport. I'm not here to get into a shouting match, but comedian George Carlin makes a great case for the superiority of baseball over football.

Baseball, says George, begins in the spring with the promise of new life.

Football begins in the fall when everything is dying.

Football is concerned with downs, as in "What down is it?"

Baseball is concerned with ups, as in "I'm not up. You're up!"

Football has hitting, clipping, piling on, spearing, personal fouls, and unnecessary roughness.

Baseball has the sacrifice.

When the score is tied at the end of the game in football, you have sudden death.

When the score is tied at the end of a baseball game, you have extra innings.

George's thoughtful analysis of baseball versus football confirms why this sport is superior to football or any other major sport in this country. I like the fact that it's not militaristic like football, where teams like the Oakland Raiders "march" down the field, "steamrolling" the opposition and "blitzing" the opposing quarterback, hoping to "sack" him.

Baseball is a game of skill and precision—delivering the pitch exactly where you want it in the strike zone while the batter tries to swing and meet the ball just so. Did you know that the difference between a long out and a home run is just one-eighth of an inch of contact between the ball and the bat?

Baseball is played in the springtime and the summertime on freshly mowed lawns and well-raked infields, its boundaries lined in the whitest of white lime. My favorite game of the year always happens on Opening Day, which symbolizes the ceremonial and symbolic end of winter and the start of spring. I love the pageantry and optimism associated with the first day of the baseball season. Life is magnified on Opening Day. The sky is a deeper blue. The grass is a little greener. When the Marine Corps Color Guard marches in and both teams stand respectfully on the baselines, I feel a sense of renewal as well. Perhaps it's fitting that Easter and Opening Day are always close on the calendar; the resurrection of Jesus Christ is our hope for salvation, and the start of the baseball seasons is when everyone receives a fresh start and is 0–0 in the win-loss column.

Perhaps that's why baseball rekindles feelings of youth and a simpler time before innocence was lost. I know that I think of baseball—not a violent contact sport like football—whenever I hear Psalm 23 recited at a solemn occasion. Listen to the pastoral images evoked by the soothing language of this psalm from David:

> The LORD is my shepherd, I shall not be in want.
>> He makes me lie down in green pastures,
> he leads me beside quiet waters,
>> he restores my soul.
> He guides me in paths of righteousness
>> for his name's sake.
> Even though I walk
>> through the valley of the shadow of death,
> I will fear no evil,
>> for you are with me;
> your rod and your staff,
>> they comfort me.
>
> You prepare a table before me
>> in the presence of my enemies.

You anoint my head with oil;
    my cup overflows.
Surely goodness and love will follow me
    all the days of my life,
and I will dwell in the house of the LORD
    forever.

They Said It

"You look forward to it like a birthday party when you're a kid. You think something wonderful is going to happen."

—Joe DiMaggio, on Opening Day

TAKE ME OUT TO THE BALF GAME . . .

31

Did you know that a new game has been invented that's a hybrid of baseball and golf?

As Yogi Berra would say, "Neither did I until I heard about it."

The game is called *balf*, which comes from a combination of BAseball and goLF. It was invented about ten years ago by Mark Schuster of Crafton, Pennsylvania.

The new game isn't as awkward as its name. Balf is played on golf courses using regulation golf balls and special wooden bats—produced by Hillerich & Bradsby, maker of the "Louisville Slugger"—called *clats*. (The name clats from CLub and bAT, get it?)

At any rate, the player stands on the tee box, tosses the golf ball into the air, and swings his clat—a long, thin-barreled baseball bat. Hopefully, his "tee shot" lands in the fairway, where the player picks up the ball again and smacks it toward the hole, except on par–3s, of course. Once the player is on the green, he uses a special clat with a putter head attached to the end of the bat, I mean clat. You stroke the ball into the hole and count up your shots.

Balf has a small hard-core audience of players, mainly on the East Coast. I hear that Brooks Robinson and Tony Oliva, great players from the 1960s, have given the game a go. Although Mark Schuster is billing balf as the new "Sport of the Third Millennium," I have my doubts, but that's okay.

Personally, balf would be pretty hard for me since I would have to toss up the golf ball while keeping the bat in my right hand. But maybe Jonathan can try it someday.

Back to the Future

All this talk about golf, however, has me thinking about the direction each game is taking. I love golf, play it one-handed, and enjoy a good walk spoiled, as Mark Twain would say. But golf's technological advances in the last decade could make the great old courses obsolete. Players with titanium-juiced drivers and souped-up balls have made the three-hundred-yard drive a routine event. The average driving distance at the 2003 Phoenix Open was 301 yards, and the driving distance on the PGA tour has increased by twenty yards or 10 percent since 1980.

Course designers and tournament directors are tired of the pros hitting driver/pitching wedge into four-hundred-yard holes or driver/seven iron into *par–5s!* The only alternative is to lengthen courses, like Augusta National did, to fend off the long-hitting pros.

Many of golf's traditionalists say it's the ball that's causing all the extra yardage. The Titleist ProV1x has sixty fewer dimples than normal balls (332 to 392), which causes it to fly further and get more roll.

The reason I'm telling you this is to show you how Major League Baseball has not changed much with the times. Sure, there's been some tinkering—lowering the mound, bringing in fences, better gloves—but by and large, today's game is not much different from the game played fifty or seventy-five years ago. The reason is because two pieces of equipment central to the game—the bat and the baseball—have stayed pretty much the same.

The last time the baseball changed was at the end of the "dead ball" era, which lasted from 1900–1919. Up until then, baseballs were as firm as pillows—and you could hit one just as far. Frank "Home Run" Baker received his nickname because he was the game's most powerful slugger, leading or tying for the league lead in home runs for four consecutive seasons from 1911–14. But get this—Frank never hit more than *twelve* home runs in a season. That's a bad month for Barry Bonds these days.

So Major League Baseball began producing baseballs that could really be called "hard balls" with the start of the 1920 season—and during the Roaring Twenties, exciting players like Babe Ruth, Lou Gehrig, Mel Ott, and Rogers Hornsby began hitting forty or more home runs in the seasons. Now, I understand that some baseball pundits think that today's ball is "juiced," which would explain why Roger Maris's 61 home-run record has been topped six times since 1998 by Mark McGwire, Sammy Sosa, and Barry Bonds. I think we're seeing more home runs because of the dilution of pitching talent (there's only so much to go around with thirty teams) and the way all the fences have been brought in at the new ballparks.

But let's turn our attention to where Major League Baseball understood that the game could have changed dramatically if it had allowed a certain piece of equipment to become part of the game. I'm talking about the aluminum bat.

Back when I was pitching college ball in the mid–1970s for Youngstown University, I started to see players coming up to the plate with these newfangled bats made out of aluminum. I noticed something whenever a strong hitter came to the plate twirling an aluminum bat in his hand: my infield and outfield backed up a few steps.

I didn't get to back up, of course, since I had to straddle the rubber before each pitch. But after a while, I understood why my infielders and outfielders wanted more space between them and the batter: the ball just shot off those aluminum bats. Baseball has changed at the amateur level since aluminum bats were formally approved in 1976: batting averages increased, as well as home runs and runs scored.

Aluminum bats are lighter than wooden bats, which means that batters can generate more bat speed during a swing. More bat speed means more bat velocity on the pitch, which explains why my teammates played deep. The ball "trampolines" off the aluminum bat because the aluminum deforms upon contact but immediately springs back. When a ball and a wooden bat collide, the wood doesn't spring back and catapult the ball.

I understand why Little Leagues and high schools and colleges want to use aluminum bats—they're cheaper in the long run than wooden bats, which break often. You can get two seasons out of an aluminum bat, where a wooden bat can break in a game or two.

You won't find aluminum bats in professional baseball, and that's a great decision. Not only would it be dangerous for a pitcher to face a Sammy Sosa with an aluminum bat in his hand, you'd have to replace outfield fences with Green Monster-like walls to keep baseballs in the park. The game would fundamentally change.

As with anything, change must be thought through before it's approved, and I'm glad that baseball is going with tradition, not expediency.

And That One Goes . . . Foul

One time during the baseball off-season, Jack Nicklaus was playing golf with Ken Griffey Jr. somewhere in Florida.

On the first tee, Jack split the fairway with a beautiful drive. Then Junior stepped onto the tee box. Like many baseball players who play golf, Junior can really hit the pill a long way. On this morning, however, he snap-hooked a drive into the adjacent fairway.

As the twosome jumped into a golf cart, the great Nicklaus couldn't help but tweak the young upstart. "In our game," he said to Junior, "we have to play our foul balls."

They Said It

"No thanks. I don't drink."

—Jeff Stone, San Francisco Giant infielder when asked
if he would like a shrimp cocktail

THE SOLOMON-LIKE DECISION 32

It was nice to see King Solomon back on the nation's sports pages.

I mean, here's a guy who was "living large" long before the term was ever invented. Three thousand years ago Solomon was the wealthiest man alive, a stud who controlled the entire region west of the Euphrates to the Mediterranean. His crowning achievement was construction of the holy temple in Jerusalem, where he inaugurated a massive public works program, building homes, vineyards, gardens, parks, orchards, and the reservoirs necessary to irrigate his plantations. His herds and flocks outnumbered anything the world had ever seen. He owned 12,000 horses with horsemen and 1,400 chariots. Solomon was quite the ladies' man, taking 700 wives and 300 concubines. The guy could also write: he composed 1,005 songs and 3,000 proverbs containing nuggets of wisdom that are read today by millions of people.

Solomon is best remembered for his wisdom as a judge, particularly in the case of the two women (prostitutes, actually) who came before him, both claiming to be the mother of an infant. After hearing each woman swear that the child was hers, Solomon pulled out a sword from its sheath and said, "Divide the child in two and give half to each woman!"

The woman who was really the mother cried out, "No, sir! Give her the child—don't kill him."

The other woman agreed with Solomon's decision. "I'm fine with that," she said. "Divide it between us, and then the child will be neither hers nor mine."

That's when Solomon knew the first woman was the real mother.

This famous story was invoked by the media when San Francisco Judge Kevin McCarthy ruled that two men fighting over ownership of Barry Bonds's 73d home-run ball had to split the estimated $1,000,000 that the ball would sell for on the memorabilia market.

The controversy began during the final weekend of the 2001 regular season. On a Friday evening at Pac Bell Park, Barry Bonds surpassed Mark McGwire's home-run record set just three years earlier by blasting No. 71 and No. 72 against the Los Angeles Dodgers. The interesting sidebar to this story is that No. 72 ricocheted back onto the field and was presented to Bonds, which meant that *he* had a million-dollar ball in his possession, if that home run turned out to be the last of the season. Why was this ball worth potentially so much money? Precedent had been set two years earlier when collector Todd McFarlane purchased McGwire's 70th home-run ball— his final homer of the 1998 season—for $3,000,000. (Just wondering . . . how much is that ball worth today?)

Barry limited himself to a pinch-hitting role the following day, a Saturday, singling in the eighth inning. But he was back in the lineup for the Giants' final game on Sunday, October 7. In the bottom of the first, he stepped up to the plate with two outs, nobody on. Not much reason for pitcher Dennis Springer to give him anything over the plate, but the division races had been decided, so maybe Dennis was thinking that he wanted to go *mano a mano* with Barry. It wasn't like the Dodgers and the Giants were going anywhere after this game.

As Barry windmilled his bat before the 3–2 pitch, a buzz swept through the ballpark. Around 1,500 fans—99 percent male—jostled for position in the right field bleachers. The outfield seats were populated by guys in their thirties and forties with dollar signs in their eyes. They came with mitts and dreams of catching Barry's final home run of the season—and becoming financially set for life.

Two of those in the stands that afternoon were Alexander Popov and Patrick Hayashi, bachelors in their mid-thirties who lived in the Bay Area. The way Patrick figured it, he had a one-in-1,500 chance of getting his hands on Bonds's next home run, which was a lot better odds than a lottery ticket.

Alex, part of the high-tech boom in Silicon Valley, wasn't in the right field stands working on his tan. He had done his homework by going online and researching where most of Barry's blasts landed—if they didn't get wet in McCovey's Cove—when they stayed inside Pac Bell. If a Bonds's bomb didn't leave the park, it usually touched down just beyond the 365-foot sign in right center. That's where Popov and his mitt stationed themselves for Barry's first at bat. As fate would have it, Hayashi stood a few feet from Popov.

Dennis Springer was a knuckleball pitcher. (Which reminds me of an interesting tangent. When Roger Maris was going for No. 60 in his 154th game of the season to tie Babe Ruth's home-run mark, the Baltimore Orioles brought in knuckleballer Hoyt Wilhelm to face Maris in the ninth inning of a meaningless game. Both benches knew that it's nearly impossible to hit a knuckler for distance because the pitch dances up to the plate with no pace and no speed. Maris didn't get No. 60, and thus was stuck with an asterisk behind No. 61* when he hit No. 60 and 61 after game 154.) The Dodger pitcher worked Barry to a full-count, and then he laid a 75-mph dipsy-do knuckler over the plate.

Barry dropped his hands and whipped his wrists and arms through the pitch. His two-tone brown-and-cherry maplewood bat struck the horsehide square, and the ball lofted like a moon shot for right center field.

Alex Popov had a bead on the ball the whole way. He looked up into the gray sky and saw the ball coming straight toward him, as if on a line. He reached with his baseball glove and snatched the ball—it would have been a legal catch if he had been in the field of play. Videotape confirms that he caught the prized home-run ball before instant mayhem and the law of the jungle took over.

What happened next is murkier, but video shows Popov being descended upon by a mob intent on wrestling the ball away from him. A dog pile ensued as pandemonium and chaos reigned. It was clearly every man for himself, fighting for a million-dollar ball. Popov testified that he had the ball for at least forty-five seconds before it disappeared.

It took Major League security men several minutes before they arrived at the melee. "Where's the ball? Where's the ball?" they shouted as they pulled bodies away from the pile.

That's when Patrick Hayashi emerged from the scrum holding up the ball. The security team whisked him and the prized ball to the Giants ballpark offices underneath the stands for safekeeping. When a Giants official handed him a piece of paper to write down his name and address, Hayashi couldn't do it because his hands were shaking too badly for him to grip the pen.

It didn't take long for a major league controversy to boil over the Bonds home-run ball. Alexander Popov felt as if he had been robbed in broad daylight as he watched the security people escort Hayashi to safety. He began collecting phone numbers of witnesses who agreed that he had had the ball in his possession, and reporters and news crews in the stands sensed there was a story brewing. Thus began the legal battle over the ownership of the No. 73 ball. Of course, it helped that Barry didn't homer in his next three at bats: he singled in the third, popped out to right in the sixth, and flied out to center in the eighth inning.

During the off-season, the Bonds home-run ball story began to develop a life of its own. More than a few pundits noted the irony that the son of a Russian immigrant who had done forced labor for the Nazis during World War II had filed a lawsuit against the son of Japanese-Americans who had been taken against their will and shipped to internment camps during World War II. Looking for proof that their two sons were totally Americanized, right?

So, sue me!

I'll see you in court, buddy.

Popov and Hayashi's protracted court case was closely followed by the baseball media. In four pretrial conferences, Popov and

Hayashi could not agree on the disposition of the ball, meaning that they couldn't agree on the money.

Judge Kevin McCarthy heard the case to its conclusion, with witnesses and dispositions and arguments and rebuttal. In the end, the judge decided that Popov and Hayashi each had an equal claim to the ball. He ordered it to be sold and the proceeds divided between the two of them—and the armies of lawyers representing them, I presume.

"King Solomon Split: Judge Divides Home-run Ball" was a typical headline following the decision announcement. News leads and sportscasters intoned in grave voices that Judge McCarthy's ruling evoked "the wisdom of Solomon."

I'm glad old King Solomon relevant again in our secular society, but the whole thing leaves me depressed. All that time, money, and legal effort spent on a home-run souvenir—aargh! The Bonds home-run ball was sold in the summer of 2003 for $517,000. After paying $67,000 in commission fees, Popov and Hayashi split $450,000. My guess is that at the end of the day, when all legal fees were paid, the pair ended with nothing to show for their legal battle.

This sordid mess reminds me of what Solomon wrote in the first chapter of Ecclesiastes: "History merely repeats itself. Nothing is truly new; it has all been done and said before. What can you point to that is new?"

It would have been interesting if Judge McCarthy had *really* invoked Solomon's famous decision regarding the baby belonging to the two mothers. What if he had ordered that the Barry Bonds 73rd home-run ball be sawed in half?

I would have liked to have been there when that happened. Would either Alexander Popov or Patrick Hayashi have rushed forward and screamed, "No, Your Honor! Don't do that!"

They Said It

"It's a curse, getting that ball. And what do you do with
the ball anyway? You can't wear it around your neck. You
can't leave it in your apartment. Someone could steal it,
or the dog could eat it. So you sell it, and people call
you greedy . . . or you don't sell it, and you're a fool.
I'm telling you, it's a curse."

—Ray Scarbosio, a friend of Alexander Popov

DON'T LOOK BACK   33

If Yogi Berra was the one catcher I would have loved to have pitched
to, then Satchel Paige is the one pitcher I would have loved to have
seen straddling the mound and mowing down batters in his prime.
Some baseball historians claim that he was the best pitcher ever.

"Ol' Satch," as they called him back in the days when he played
in the Negro Leagues seventy-five years ago, was a string bean right-
hander known for his famous "hesitation pitch." Satchel would go
into his windup, make a deliberate hitch and stop moving for the
longest second or two, then unleash a pea-sized fastball called the
"Long Tom" on the unsuspecting hitter. Satchel had other pitches in
his repertoire: "the barber" came in right underneath the batter's

chin; the "two-hump blooper" guaranteed a ground ball to the infield, and the "jump ball," the "trouble ball," and the "long ball" befuddled batters from Maine to Mexico City. Sometimes he went into a double or triple windup before fashioning a huge leg kick; that was known as the "Step 'n Pitch-it."

He was blazing fast—so fast that Yankee great Joe DiMaggio said he never faced anyone who threw faster. Ol' Satch was deadly accurate as well. According to one story, he threw twenty straight pitches over a chewing gum wrapper that had been laid across home plate. Folklore has it that in one Negro League game, Paige called in his outfielders to sit behind the mound while he struck out the side in nine pitches. "More fabulous tales have been told of Satchel's pitching ability than of any other pitcher in organized baseball," said New York baseball writer Tom Meany.

Satchel was born Leroy Paige on July 7, 1906, but that date is just a general estimate, which only adds to his mysteriousness. No one really knew how old he was when he played. Satchel earned his nickname as a young boy when he carried bags and satchels for passengers at railroad depots. He began pitching as a young boy, but since this was the Jim Crow era, black ballplayers were barred from organized baseball. His only option was playing in the Negro Leagues. Satchel signed with the Kansas City Monarchs and quickly established himself as a gate attraction. People just had to come out and see Satchel perform from the mound! He did wondrous things: pitching 64 consecutive scoreless innings, winning 21 consecutive decisions, and during the 1933 season, compiling a 31–4 record.

During the winter months, Satchel and other Negro League All-Stars barnstormed the country playing exhibitions against white All-Star teams stocked with major league stars like Joe DiMaggio. I can only imagine what was going through Satchel's mind as he blew the ball by the overmatched white stars—injustice?—but he appeared not to let anything bother him. I'm sure the "color line" did bother Satch; he wouldn't be human if it didn't. Many of the Negro League teams played in hand-me-down big league uniforms, which, when you stop and think about it, was just one more indignity that had to be swallowed. Satchel's dream was to one day play in a *real* major league uniform and pitch on baseball's grandest stage.

Satchel had a second strike against him as well: he was also pitching against Father Time. Every year that he toiled in the Negro Leagues added one more year to his arm and to his age—however old he was. Would he be too old ever to get his chance? Following World War II, when rumors swept through Negro League baseball that the big leagues were close to breaking the "color" barrier, Satchel wondered if he would be the one. After all, he was the most famous Negro League player and a legend on the barnstorming circuit, or baseball's "chitlins" circuit. But all the overnight traveling on wheezing buses, grabbing a few hours of sleep in "coloreds only" second-rate hotels, and playing in threadbare bandboxes took their toll.

Branch Rickey, the Brooklyn Dodgers general manager, knew all about this legendary pitcher from the Negro League, but he passed on Ol' Satch for a couple of reasons: he felt time had passed him by and that his showmanship wouldn't be appropriate in the serious business of breaking the color barrier. Rickey decided that Jackie Robinson would become the first black to play in the major leagues in 1947. As I said earlier when I picked him for my All-Time All-Star team, Jackie endured the most vile treatment during his rookie season, so Rickey probably made the right call.

Satchel later wrote in his autobiography that being passed over for Jackie hurt him deeply. "I'd been the guy who'd started all that big talk about letting us in the big time. I'd been the one who'd opened up the major league parks to the colored teams. I'd been the one who the white boys wanted to barnstorm against. I'd been the one who everybody had said should be in the majors."

I feel for the guy. Satchel paid his dues in triplicate, toiling in the Negro Leagues and barnstorming during the off-season for nearly twenty-five years. Once Jackie paved the way, however, they couldn't keep Ol' Satch out of the big leagues for too long. Although he missed his opportunity to be the "great integrator," as some pundits called it, Satchel's dream came true a year later.

During the midst of the 1948 season, the Cleveland Indians needed extra pitching for the pennant race against the New York Yankees. Bill Veeck—yes, the same guy who once sent midgets to the plate and lowered and raised outfield fences—looked to Ol' Satch. But Veeck wanted to be sure that all these legendary stories were true—like pitching strikes over gum wrappers. So Veeck gave Satchel a tryout and tossed a cigarette on the ground. "Use that as home plate," said Veeck. Satchel fired five fastballs, and all but one sailed directly over the cigarette.

Veeck signed the famous barnstormer to a contract, but some said that this was another one of Veeck's famous publicity stunts. After all, this guy had to be what—fifty years old? (He was thought to be forty-two years old.) Wasn't he born during the Civil War? But when Satchel made his first appearance—in relief—in Cleveland, the Indian fans stood and gave him a ten-minute ovation, saluting him for his long-deserved achievement of making it to the big leagues. Not long after that, Satchel started his first major league game on August 3, 1948, before 72,652 fans at Cleveland's Municipal Stadium, a new attendance record for a major league night game.

Ol' Satch responded by twirling a dazzling complete game shutout, and that silenced any remaining critics. In just half a season, he registered a 6–1 record with a glittering 2.48 ERA, but more importantly, he helped pitch the Indians to a pennant and a World Series victory that year. That fall, there was some talk about Satchel being named "Rookie of the Year" in the American League, which was a farce, since Satchel was well beyond forty years old.

Father Time eventually proved to be too formidable for Ol' Satch. Well past his prime, he hung on for a few years, and he was even reunited with Bill Veeck in St. Louis when he signed to play for the Browns in 1951. Ol' Satch relaxed in his own personal rocking chair in the bullpen provided for him by Veeck when he wasn't pitching and cultivated an image of an old coot. After dozing in his rocking chair, he'd wake up and issue proverbs such as, "If your stomach disputes you, lie down and pacify it with cool thoughts," or his most famous saying: "Don't look back. Something might be gaining on you."

Satch didn't look back, but time overtook him. Ol' Satch barnstormed well into his fifties, and then he became the *oldest* player to ever appear in a major league game when he was brought back to pitch three innings for the Kansas City A's against the Boston Red Sox on September 25, 1965. Sure, it was another Charlie O. Finley stunt, but at the age of fifty-nine, Satchel acquitted himself well on the mound that day. He walked off the mound with his head high.

Major League Baseball attempted to even the scales three years later. It seems that Ol' Satch was just 158 days short of qualifying for a Major League pension. The Atlanta Braves agreed to let him suit up with the team and rock in his bullpen rocking chair until he qualified for his pension. That was a nice gesture, but it was topped when Satchel—who played less than five years in the majors—was voted into the Baseball Hall of Fame in 1971. "This is the proudest day of my life," he said.

Satchel's remarkable story reminds me of the parable that Jesus told in Matthew 20 about the owner of an estate who went out early one morning to hire workers to harvest his fields. The owner found a few workers at the hiring hall waiting for jobs, so he sent them into his fields, telling him that he would pay them for a day's work at the end of the day. The field owner hired more men at noon and at three o'clock in the afternoon, sending them out to work his fields.

At sunset, he called everyone in. He gave *everyone* the same daily wage—let's call it fifty dollars—but the workers who started early in the morning protested, saying they worked much longer than the guys who strolled in at three o'clock.

"Friend," he answered one of them. "I did you no wrong. Didn't you agree to work all day for fifty dollars? Take the money and go.

That's what we agreed to, and I can pay my laborers anything I want."

Jesus told this parable to illustrate God's generosity regarding salvation. When we die and go to heaven, there will be people there who became Christians when they were in Vacation Bible School, and there will be people there who repented of their sins on their deathbeds and accepted Christ into their hearts. Each received the priceless gift of eternal life and a heavenly crown of glory, even if some did not "work" in the fields very long.

If you look at Satchel Paige's Major League career, he compiled a modest 28–31 record and a 3.29 ERA in less than five seasons. He arrived at the vineyard late in life—three o'clock, if you will—through no fault of his own. He deserved to get paid the same as everyone else, and that's why Satchel Paige deserves to be in the Hall.

They Said It

"I never threw an illegal pitch. The trouble is, once in a while I would toss one that ain't never been seen by this generation."

—Satchel Paige, ageless pitcher

THE FEARED CLOSER

When I came up, relief pitchers were called "firemen"—pitchers called in to extinguish late-inning fires. (Relievers who couldn't hold a lead were known as "arsonists.") At any rate, Goose Gossage was our go-to guy on the Padres when the opposing team had men on second and third base with the game on the line. It didn't matter if it was the seventh, eighth, or ninth inning: if the skipper felt we needed Goose in there, he got the ball. It didn't hurt that he looked so mean on the mound with that shaggy Fu Manchu moustache and imposing build.

Relief aces don't put out fires anymore. Instead, they've become "closers" who start off the ninth inning with nobody on and nobody out. All they need is three outs, and they have another "save." When Antonio Alfonseca of the Chicago Cubs led the majors with forty-five saves in 2000, he never entered a game with the tying run on base.

Today's prototypical closer is Trevor Hoffman of the Padres. It's exciting to watch him enter the game in the top of ninth in front of a big home crowd. Trevor jogs purposely from the left field bullpen to the mound with AC/DC's "Hell's Bells" blaring through the PA system. As he takes his eight warm-up pitches, you feel as psyched as he does. It's "Trevor Time."

But Trevor—like 95 percent of today's closers—usually comes into the game with a clean slate: ninth inning, no one on base, and the first batter swinging a bat with a leaded doughnut in the one-deck circle. The Padres have a one-, two-, or three-run lead, which makes it a save "opportunity." (If the lead is four runs or more, Trevor won't qualify for a save, so then he won't pitch.) In other words, the table is set like Maxim's restaurant on the Rue Royale in Paris. I'm not saying that it's easy to get a save in those situations, but

Trevor did collect fifty-three consecutive saves in 1998 to tie the National League record.

Since Trevor never comes in until the ninth inning, he's developed a routine right out of *Groundhog Day:*

- For the first four innings, Trevor sits in the bullpen with his buddies and spits sunflower seeds into the dirt.
- At the beginning of the fifth inning, he gets up and heads into the clubhouse. He listens to the game on the radio while he cleans his cleats and takes a shower. The hot water on his right arm helps him get loose.
- During the sixth and seventh innings, Trevor stretches and works out with his trainer.
- By the end of the seventh inning, Trevor returns to the bullpen. For road games, he waits until the eighth inning.
- If the Padres are ahead in the eighth inning, he expects the phone call from the Padre bench telling him to get warm.
- Ninth inning—"Hell's Bells" and Trevor Time!

Dave Stewart, once the Padres' pitching coach, said this about the mentality of closers: "You want to be that guy. You want to be the pitcher who closes it down. You want to put your foot on their neck. I guess it would almost be like an assassin's mentality. Trevor has it for sure."

Setting them down one, two, three may sound like easy work, but it's not. Games can turn quickly on a pitch or two. Closers have a short shelf life because if you start blowing leads, you're suddenly relegated to "long relief" or "setup" duty—for the new closer. It helps to have a short memory.

Pitching no more than one inning in a save situation is one more way that the modern game has evolved; today's cast of closers throws around half the innings that Goose used to throw twenty years ago. Yet for this latest "advance" in the game, teams are no more successful at protecting leads late in the game than they were in my day.

According to the Elias Sports Bureau, teams taking a one-run lead into the ninth inning won 83.9 percent of the games in 2000; in 1990, that figure was 86.4 percent, and in 1980, 84.7 percent.

It still takes a special guy to close the door when the other team is down to its final three outs. Many closers are intimidating fire-ballers with a steely glare. Eric Gagne of the Los Angeles Dodgers wears goofy goggles and a wild goatee that hitters find downright menacing. Troy Percival of the Anaheim Angels, who looks as if he has a perpetual two-day beard, squints and goes after batters with high heat. Robb Nen of the San Francisco Giants is another intim-idator, and Atlanta's John Smoltz has actually gotten faster since he came off "Tommy John" surgery in 2000. Smoltz and Eric Gagne share the National League record with fifty-five saves. Other closers, however, rely on guile and keeping hitters off balance. Trevor Hoff-man's go-to pitch is the change-up; his fastball rarely tops 90 mph these days. John Franco's out pitch is his sinker ball.

What today's closers have in common are titanium nerves and a love for fierce competition. They want the ball when it's time to close the books. They are paid to save the day. Great closers remind me of today's great evangelists—those men who can stand up before an audience and "seal the deal." They are the ones at the revival meetings or the evangelistic outreaches carrying a Bible in one hand and exhorting their audience with the other. They are the ones say-ing words like these:

> I want you to imagine a huge wall that divides this room. On one side of the wall is where God lives, and on the other side of the wall is where you live. That wall, or barrier, is what the Bible refers to as sin. Romans 3:23 says, "For all have sinned and fall short of the glory of God." In other words, we are all brought into the world separated from God. In Romans, we are told that the wages of sin is separation from God and eternal death, but God loved us so much that he provided a way, a way at great expense.

The door that he provided in the wall was his Son, Jesus Christ. All of us who were born separated from God by this barrier can now come to Christ and know him in a personal way. Jesus says in Revelation 3:20, "Here I am! I stand at the door and knock. If anyone hears my voice and opens the door, I will come in and eat with him, and he with me." God is knocking at the door of your heart, saying, *Follow Me . . . come and follow Me.*

Have you ever heard a "closer" like that? Just a question, but did this closer seal the deal for you?

They Said It

"All of his saves have come in relief appearances."

—Ralph Kiner, New York Mets announcer

CLOSING THE DEAL   35

Bobby Richardson is one of the best evangelistic "closers" I've ever met. Here's a guy who played twelve seasons at second base for the New York Yankees during the 1950s and 1960s, but when he retired from baseball, he didn't buy a house on a golf course and start working on his short game. Instead, he devoted himself to Christian out-reach. Bobby became president of the Baseball Chapel Ministry and shared the gospel with anyone in baseball who'd listen. We won't know how many he led to the Lord until we go to heaven.

One of those persons whom Bobby pursued for Jesus was his teammate Mickey Mantle, probably the biggest star of the 1950s. In the early days of television, Mickey played for the nation's most famous team in the most famous ballpark in an era when baseball overshadowed every professional sport. Mickey, a golden-haired country boy from Oklahoma blessed with lumberjack forearms and blazing speed, was a switch-hitting power hitter. His prodigious home runs were the first to be called "tape-measure" shots. He is reputed to have hit the longest measured home run in a major league game when he clobbered a chest-high fastball that cleared the left field bleachers at Griffith Stadium, home of the Washington Sena-tors. That "monster blast of all time" just missed the National Bohemian beer sign before bouncing on Oakdale Place NW, 565 feet from home plate. Another Mantle explosion happened at Yan-kee Stadium, where his shot kept climbing until it struck the park's right field façade. If the ball had kept sailing, it would have landed 602 feet from home plate, or so people say.

Mickey didn't hang out much with Bobby, mainly because Bobby didn't fortify his diet with generous amounts of adult bever-ages, and they went their separate ways after they both retired from baseball.

But Bobby didn't give up. For three decades, he shared the good news of Jesus Christ with his former teammate whenever their paths crossed. Mickey was more interested in playing golf with his buddies and boozing at the 19th hole, however, than in thinking through what Bobby said. The Commerce Comet, as Mickey was nick-named, appeared in public in an inebriated state so often that radio DJ Don Imus quipped, "Drop by Mantle's restaurant about two any morning, and try to guess which table Mantle's under."

Mickey hit rock bottom in 1994 and checked himself into the Betty Ford Center in Palm Desert, California, for alcohol rehab. He vowed to never take a drink again, and it looked as if he had turned his life around. But forty years of drinking had damaged his liver, so much so that Mickey needed a liver transplant, or he would die. He was fortunate to receive an immediate liver transplant. For a man in his early sixties, it looked as if he would have many more years to watch his grandchildren grow up.

After receiving this new lease on life, Mickey called Bobby Richardson as he recuperated in the hospital. Bobby's wife, Betsy, was also on the line. She told Mickey, "I know how much you appreciate the organ donation and the opportunity to live longer, but I want to think of this as God's gift to you, Mickey, because this is just a reprieve. God loves you, and he wants to spend eternity with you."

While Mickey was recuperating in the hospital, he was stricken with searing abdominal pain. Doctors at Baylor University Medical Center in Texas probed and prodded the former Yankee until they discovered that cancer had aggressively spread to his vital organs. Bad news for Mickey: he was terminal.

I have to credit the Mick because he called in his closer. Bobby and Betsy were asked to fly out from their South Carolina home to visit Mickey in the hospital in Dallas. When the Richardsons knocked lightly on the hospital door, they were ushered to the wan-looking patient inside the private room. On this summer day in 1995, Mickey Mantle—his once-strong body overwhelmed by cancer cells in his lungs, heart cavity, and other vital organs—lay at death's door.

Bobby was ready to deliver his final pitch, to ask Mickey if he wanted to accept Christ into his heart and know that he would be united with him in heaven, when Mickey stopped him. "Bobby, I wanted to tell you that I have trusted Christ to be my Savior."

Bobby felt a tremendous weight fall from his shoulders, but like any good closer, he wanted to be sure. He walked through the Four Spiritual Laws with Mickey.

"Did you acknowledge that Jesus Christ is the Son of God and that he came on this earth to die for our sins?"

"Yes, I did," replied Mickey.

"Did you acknowledge that you are a sinner?"

"Yes, I did."

"Did you ask for forgiveness of your sins?"

"Yes."

"And did you ask Jesus Christ into your heart so that you can spend eternity with him?"

"Yes, I did, Bobby."

That was it—Bobby's relief appearance was over. Mickey had asked for and received the forgiveness he so desperately needed. He had been helped by a former teammate who had taken the time to show how much he cared for Mickey Mantle.

Mickey's Turn to Sign

Before he became a Christian on his deathbed, Mickey Mantle liked to tell a funny story about his death and arrival at the Pearly Gates, where St. Peter somberly looked inside his book to see if Mickey's name was written there. He shook his head no, and the crestfallen Mickey turned to leave.

"Oh, before you go," St. Peter said, "God wants to know if you'll sign these six dozen balls."

When Mickey received his coronation on August 13, 1995, there were no baseballs waiting for his autograph. Instead, the King of kings greeted Mickey with open arms to thunderous applause, like none Mickey had ever heard in Yankee Stadium.

They Said It

"Very few people take your breath away, but that was the effect Mickey had. He was truly a great American hero."

—Billy .Crystal, actor and director of *61**

THE HOLLYWOOD DARLING

Bo Belinsky and I were both left-handers and had jet black hair, and each of us pitched eight seasons in the big leagues. But that's where our similarities end.

Bo broke in with the Los Angeles Angels in 1962, the year after the expansion team joined the American League. The Angels played their games at Chavez Ravine when the Dodgers weren't in town.

Baseball was new to Los Angeles and the Hollywood crowd in the early 1960s, and they fell in love with each other. The stars and starlets from films and TV hobnobbed with the players before and after the games: Milton Berle, Bob Hope, Jack Benny, Esther Williams, and Jayne Mansfield were just a few of the celebrities drawn to the bright lights of Chavez Ravine.

Bo Belinsky was just an old rookie—twenty-five years old—who had been drafted by the expansion club. Early feature stories painted the picture of a career minor league player who made more money hustling pool than playing professional baseball. Not only was he an artist with the pool cue, but he liked playing cards and the ponies. "We knew when we drafted him that Bo was a character," said Irv Kaze, the Angel's publicist. "What we didn't know was, could he pitch?"

Bo was what my wife, Jan, would call a charmer—a guy on the make. If he had worn a black leather jacket, he would have been a ringer for James Dean, the Hollywood icon of the 1950s who died in a mysterious auto accident. Bo preferred sharp clothes—expensive tailored suits, a gold watch, cool shades, and suede shoes. This suave-looking guy looked as if he was hanging out with the Vegas "Rat Pack"—Frank, Sammy, and Dean.

He created some buzz when he won three games in the first month of the season to run his win-loss record to 3–0. Then came his brush with immortality: on May 5, 1962 at Chavez Ravine, Bo Belinsky pitched the first major league no-hitter in California, blanking the Baltimore Orioles, 2–0.

What Bo didn't tell reporters after that game was that he had woken up ten hours earlier at the crack of noon next to a woman he picked up at Sunset Strip nightclub. The ladies' man was what my son would call a "chick magnet." He cruised the L.A. nightclub scene in his candy-apple red Cadillac convertible, staying up until the wee hours with female attention on his arms.

After pitching that no-hitter in front of the hometown folks, Bo was the toast of the town, the world his oyster. He dated a succession of Hollywood starlets: Mamie Van Doren, Tina Louise, Juliet Prowse, Connie Stevens, and Ann Margaret. He appeared on TV shows and got invited to all the big Hollywood parties. Everybody wanted to be near him. Some say he was the first "outlaw jock" of our times, the kind of anti-hero that the rebellious Sixties ushered in.

And then it all went *poof*. Like the carriage that turned back into a pumpkin at the stroke of midnight, whatever stuff Bo had on his pitches that May night against Baltimore couldn't be summoned very often after that no-hitter. "When I stepped out on Sunset Boulevard after that game, I should've made a left. Instead, I made a right," he said. He adopted the persona of a heavy-drinking, pool-hustling playboy, and that label stuck to him like flypaper. Although his pitching effectiveness eroded, Bo managed to hang around the majors for eight seasons. His lifetime record was a forgettable 28–51 when he retired in 1970. "Bo Belinsky had a million-dollar arm and a ten-cent head," said Buzzie Bavasi, Los Angeles Dodger vice president, shaking his head.

Out of baseball, Bo tried to settle down. He married a *Playboy* centerfold model, Jo Collins, but that union ended in divorce. He then married heiress Janie Weyerhaeuser, which produced twin daughters in 1976, but that marriage ended in divorce shortly after the twins were born. Bo hit rock bottom that same year when he woke up under a freeway bridge, hung over and holding an empty bottle of Japanese sake in his pitching hand. To his credit, he stopped drinking cold turkey and began to grow up.

Flash forward more than twenty years, and Bo has moved to Las Vegas, where he's in his early sixties and selling used cars for a living. Bo comes down with bladder cancer, and that's when he has a conversion experience and becomes a born-again Christian. "Can you imagine that I had to come to Las Vegas to find Jesus Christ?" he later said.

For the first time, Bo felt peace—in what he was doing and where he was going. He was like the prodigal son who left the family estate and spent his inheritance on wine, women, and the fast life. If Bo were alive today—the cancer got him in 2001—he'd tell you that he ate from the pig's trough for too many years before he came to his senses. But when Bo came back over the hill, his Father saw him coming from a long distance away and was filled with loving pity. He ran and embraced him and kissed him.

We're told in Luke 15 that when the prodigal son protested, saying that he had sinned against heaven and his father and that he was not worthy to be called his son, his father would have none of it. His father ordered the servants to bring the finest robe in the house and put it on his son, and a jeweled ring for his finger and a nice pair of shoes. "We must celebrate with a feast, for this son of mine was dead and has returned to life. He was lost and is found," said the father (Luke 15:23–24, TLB).

Bo Belinsky once was lost, but then he found Jesus Christ.

They Said It

> "If I'd known I was gonna pitch a no-hitter today,
> I would have gotten a haircut."

—Bo Belinsky, following his no-hitter on May 5, 1962

> "How can a guy win a game if you don't give
> him any runs?"

—Bo Belinsky, after losing a game 15–0

FAMILY FEUD   37

Clubhouse clashes are as old as the game. When you put two dozen highly competitive, high-strung, and highly opinionated ballplayers in the same room for longer than sixty seconds, you're going to have conflicts crop up sooner or later.

Sometimes intramural spats begin innocently. When Roberto Alomar didn't like the way Mets teammate Roger Cedeño teased him about the pencil-thin moustache that Roberto sported on his 1988 rookie baseball card, the two rushed each other and had to be separated by Mo Vaughn, which was quite a separation.

Chad Curtis, the "Iron Chipmunk" (and a fine Christian brother) who played on several teams during the 1990s, was involved in several clubhouse scrapes during his career. Chad wasn't afraid to let his teammates know that he didn't like their gangsta rap music blaring at 150 decibels in the clubhouse. This attitude didn't endear him to certain members of the team, however. One time, when Chad said something to the effect of "Turn it down!", Kevin Mitchell pushed him into a Ping-Pong table, and all hell broke loose. Another clubhouse scuffle occurred when Chad complained out loud about Royce Clayton's boom box, which happened to be blaring "The Thong Song" while children were walking through the clubhouse before game time. He and Clayton had to be separated before they came to blows as well.

I wasn't immune to clubhouse friction when I played in the big leagues. I'll never forget the 1988 season when I played for the San Francisco Giants. I and three other pitchers—Scott Garrelts, Jeff Brantley, and Atlee Hammaker—had been up front about being believers, and we did not hide our faith under a bushel. The beat writers, always looking for something to write about, coined a term for our quartet: the "God Squad." They might as well have painted bull's-eyes on the back of our uniforms for all the good it did us. Anything and everything we said could be interpreted by our teammates as "holier than thou." If we commented that we didn't go to R-rated movies with tons of nudity and sex, then our teammates thought we were judging them. If we said that we preferred to have a Bible study in our hotel rooms after a road game, that was interpreted as being antisocial by our teammates.

After a while, the "God Squad" term became a pejorative. It certainly made life difficult for us in the clubhouse as reporters constantly probed other ballplayers about their feelings regarding the "religious" pitchers on their team. Scott, Jeff, Atlee, and I read anonymous quotes from our teammates questioning whether we had what it took to be winners. Some felt that we were too "passive" or "weak" because we shrugged off defeat, thinking it must have been "God's will."

That was a bunch of baloney because I know I fought with everything I had when I was on the mound. I *loved* the competition, but more important, I knew the batter was trying to take money out of my pocket by stroking a hit against me. Conversely, I wanted to take money out of *his* pocket by getting him out. Until I was blue in the face, I told reporters, "Listen, Jesus Christ is my example. I play for him. When I play, I play to glorify God. I recognize the ability he's given me, and so I play with everything I have."

Despite that attitude, I felt like some of the other players were boring a hole in my back whenever I walked through the clubhouse before a game. I remember quietly dressing one time when I felt someone tapping on my shoulder. I swung around, only to find a teammate with a leering grin holding a *Playboy* magazine in his hands. He turned the magazine on its side, unveiled Miss April in all her glory, and then he stuck the glossy foldout in my face.

That's the way it goes sometimes, so it shouldn't surprise anyone that personalities clash on major league ball clubs. Think about it: you have a multicultural, multiracial group of high-testosterone young men thrown together for seven, eight months a year. You're told to get along, although you travel, eat, relax, and play ball together every day and every night. If things go well, lifelong bonding relationships are formed. If things go bad, you barely tolerate each other. Worse, you openly despise each other.

Throughout baseball's history, teammates have been at each other's throats and still won pennants and World Series championships. Barry Bonds, during the midst of the 2002 season, literally grabbed Jeff Kent by the throat in a Giants dugout dust-up. They feuded for the better part of six seasons until Kent signed as a free agent with the Houston Astros in 2003.

Bonds and Kent are just the latest example of teammates who couldn't stand each other's guts. Let's take a look at a few of the memorable Hatfields versus McCoys-type conflicts over the years:

Joe Tinker Versus Johnny Evers

The particulars: Chicago Cubs shortstop and second baseman, and teammates from 1902 to 1913.

The bone of contention: We're talking Tinker-to-Evers-to-Chance, right? Two-thirds of the most storied double-play team of all time couldn't get it together off the field, however. It seems their feud started in Washington, Indiana, where the club was playing an exhibition game. Evers hailed a taxi at a hotel and left Tinker and the other teammates coughing exhaust fumes. Later, Tinker went looking for Evers, and they engaged in a fistfight on the field.

The feud: After their fight, Tinker told Evers, in so many words, "You play your position, and I'll play mine." The Hall of Fame teammates didn't speak to each other for thirty-three years. Things stayed that way until 1938, when the pair, unbeknownst to each other, was invited to help broadcast the 1938 World Series that the Cubs were playing in. After a moment of strained silence, they fell into each other's arms and cried.

Babe Ruth Versus Lou Gehrig

The particulars: No. 3 batted third and played right field, No. 4 batted cleanup and played first base. They played together on the New York Yankees from 1925 to 1934.

The bone of contention: Lou Gehrig's mother made a rude remark about Babe Ruth's wife or daughter sometime around 1934.

The feud: Someone told the Babe that Lou's mom had said something—how's that for hearing something third-hand—so the Sultan of Swat shunned Lou for five years until "Lou Gehrig Appreciation Day" on July 4, 1939 at Yankee Stadium.

The Iron Horse, ailing from ALS, was surrounded at home plate by teammates from the 1927 and 1939 Yankees. At first, it appeared that Lou couldn't summon the strength or the composure to address the sellout crowd, but he did. (I've reprinted his farewell speech at the end of this chapter.) Lou Gehrig was dying, and everyone knew it, including the Babe. They embraced again like old friends. Lou died two years later.

Dizzy Dean Versus Joe Medwick

The particulars: Ol' Diz, a pitcher, was the leader of the St. Louis Cardinals' Gas House Gang of the 1930s; Joe, a left fielder, was his teammate from 1932 to 1937.

The bone of contention: Joe, a no-nonsense player who kept his own company, didn't like the teasing he received from the court jester of the Cardinals, Dizzy Dean.

The feud: A mild one since Dizzy couldn't hold a grudge. It all depended on Medwick's mood.

Dick Allen Versus Frank Thomas

The particulars: Allen was the Phillies third baseman, while Thomas played first base and outfield. They were teammates for the 1964 and 1965 seasons.

The bone of contention: Dick Allen, a black player during the contentious civil rights days of the 1960s, thought he heard Thomas make a racist remark during batting practice. Allen punched Thomas; then Thomas returned with a bat and began pummeling Allen. Teammates saved Allen from getting his skull caved in.

The feud: It didn't last long as Thomas was waived by the Phillies front office after the game.

Don Sutton Versus Steve Garvey

The particulars: Sutton pitched for the Dodgers, while Garvey played first base. They were teammates a long time—eleven seasons from 1969 to 1980.

The bone of contention: Sutton, an ace right-hander, and Garvey, a power-hitting first baseman with Popeye arms, weren't best buds. While Garvey was popular with the fans, he did not endear himself to his teammates. Sutton went public by criticizing him in a *Washington Post* story that got picked up around the country. When Garvey read it, he confronted Sutton in the visitors' clubhouse at Shea Stadium in New York. Much finger pointing ensued, but the argument escalated when Sutton made an ill-advised comment about Garvey's wife, Cyndi. The Garv charged Sutton, and the pair rolled on the floor, hammering away at each other until teammates pulled them apart.

The feud: Sutton and Garvey caught a break—their fight happened during a newspaper strike in Los Angeles, so their feud didn't get much ink at the time. Still, they hated each other's guts for a long time.

Reggie Jackson Versus Billy Martin

The particulars: Yankee right fielder and Yankee manager during the "Bronx Zoo" era from 1977 to 1979.

The bone of contention: When Reggie joined the Yankees in 1977, he popped off to all the newspapers that he would be the "straw that stirs the drink" in New York, which caused a few eyes to roll in the Yankee clubhouse. Then he expressed his desire to have a candy bar named after him. Reggie may have wished otherwise on Opening Day when fans showered the field with free Reggie bars handed to fans as they entered Yankee Stadium. Manager Billy Martin, who told owner George Steinbrenner not to sign Reggie, didn't cotton to this newcomer. One Saturday afternoon at Fenway Park, Reggie allowed a lazy fly ball to fall in front of him. Reggie picked up the ball on one bounce and tossed it into second base. It looked like a routine single.

Wait a minute! Billy, a hustler all his life, didn't think Reggie gave it his all on the play. He immediately called time and directed a bench player to replace Reggie. Now, you never, ever replace a player in the middle of the inning, unless you want to show him up, but that's exactly what Billy wanted to do that afternoon. Reggie ran toward Billy, flapping his arms. Billy stepped out in front of the dugout and flapped his arms as well. What ensued before a nationwide television audience was a spirited scream fest between the Yankee manager and his star player. *The feud:* Hitting three home runs in Game 6 of the 1977 World Series certainly helped the pair kiss and make up, but they never became buddies. You could say the feud ended on Christmas Day in 1989 when Billy died in an auto accident.

Barry Bonds Versus Jeff Kent

The particulars: Giants left fielder and Giants second baseman, 1996 to 2002.

The bone of contention: Nobody's really sure why they didn't seem to like each other. Maybe Jeff Kent resented all the media attention that Barry received, but home-run hitters have always dominated the sports pages and brought fans to the park. Maybe Barry was tired of Kent's lip. I think the media blew their so-called feud out of proportion because they were looking for something to write about, and the truth is, there were two superstars on the same team.

The feud: Ever since Jeff joined the Astros in 2003, the feud has been put on the back burner.

Family feuds—that's what these teammate feuds can be categorized as—have been around since the First Family was on this earth. The Bible tells that Adam and Eve, after they sinned and the Big Ump in the Sky kicked them out of the Garden, started having children. Cain came first, followed by another brother named Abel. Cain became a farmer, while Abel tended to the sheep. We're told that at harvest time Cain brought the Lord a gift of his farm produce, while Abel presented fatty cuts of meat from his best lambs. The Lord accepted Abel's offering but not Cain's, which greatly bothered him. In fact, Cain got so mad that he did a Lou Piniella impersonation when he began kicking dirt on home plate. Cain was furious with God.

But God wasn't going to change his call—that Cain's sacrifice wasn't good enough. The older brother grabbed a Hillerich & Bradsby bat (I'm guessing here) from the rack and took out a few swings at Abel. Unfortunately, Cain connected and became the first member of Murderer's Row in man's history.

A family feud like this is another reminder of our sinful nature. Adam and Eve, who had a perfect game going in the Garden until they disobeyed God by eating from the Tree of Knowledge, saw how a relatively small sin—disobedience—ultimately led to an out-of-control sin—murdering a sibling.

It's best to nip these family feuds in the bud. If left unchecked, the dispute can escalate until sin takes root and something bad happens. Besides, isn't life too short to feud with another player?

Lou's Farewell Speech

Lou Gehrig, as I mentioned earlier, knew he was facing an opponent who would punch him out in the end—Death—when he addressed the sold-out crowd at Yankee Stadium on the Fourth of July in 1939. His words are emblematic of the grace with which he played this great game. The following is an excerpt from his farewell speech:

> Fans, for the past two weeks, you have been reading about a bad break I got. Yet today, I consider myself the luckiest man on the face of the earth. I have been in ballparks for seventeen years, and I have never received anything but kindness and encouragement from you fans. Look at these grand men [around me]. Which of you wouldn't consider it the highlight of his career just to associate with them for even one day?

Sure, I'm lucky. When the New York Giants, a team you would give your right arm to beat and vice versa, sends you a gift, that's something. When you have a father and mother who work all their lives so that you can have an education and build your body, it's a blessing. When you have a wife who has been a tower of strength and shown more courage than you dreamed existed, that's the finest thing I know. So I close in saying that I might have had a bad break, but I have an awful lot to live for.

I don't know if Lou Gehrig was a Christian before he died so young. In those days, any talk of religion was "private." You didn't talk about God, and if you did, you referred to him as The Man Upstairs or The Great Scorekeeper in the Sky or some other euphemism.

I hope that Lou put his trust in Christ before he passed away. He certainly had time to reflect upon eternity and what lay ahead. If he did become a believer, then he's got a new streak going—number of days in heaven. Unlike his record for playing in 2,130 consecutive games, which lasted for fifty-six years until Cal Ripken broke it, Lou's new streak will never end.

They Said It

"The Babe is one fellow, and I'm another,
and I could never be exactly like him. I don't try.
I just go on as I am in my own right."

—Lou Gehrig, on playing with Babe Ruth

BASEBALL AND
POETIC LICENSE

38

Tinker to Evers to Chance.

Although we talked about how Joe Tinker and Johnny Evers despised each other off the field in the last chapter, you have to admit that the most famous double-play combination of all time has a certain ring to it. We can credit the melodious cadence to Franklin Pierce Adams, a New York newspaper columnist who immortalized the vaunted Cubs double-play team in poetic verse about a hundred years ago. Not many people know this, but sportswriters in the early part of the twentieth century sometimes reverted to poems and poetic musings to keep their readers entertained in that pre-*SportsCenter* era.

Adams wrote his famous poem about Tinker to Evers to Chance from the point of view of his readers—New York Giants fans. I've reprinted it below, and keep in mind that the term "gonfalon" refers to a flag or pennant. Thus, the phrase "pricking our gonfalon bubble" means that the Cubs' ability to come up with the key double-play team ended the Giants' hopes of winning the National League pennant.

Baseball's Sad Lexicon

These are the saddest of possible words:
"Tinker to Evers to Chance."
Trio of bear cubs, and fleeter than birds,
Tinker and Evers and Chance.
Ruthlessly pricking our gonfalon bubble
Making a Giant hit into a double—
Words that are heavy with nothing but trouble:
"Tinker to Evers to Chance."

The funny thing is that Tinker to Evers to Chance did not turn that many double plays, at least compared to the modern game. Then again, this was the dead ball era, which keyed on the bunt, hit-and-run, and stolen bases. Infields were drawn in to get the runner at home, not play for the double-play ball.

Tinker to Evers to Chance. It rolls off your tongue like . . . like . . . Matthew, Mark, Luke, and John. Don't you feel warm inside when you say, "Matthew, Mark, Luke, and John?" I do, and it feels like everything is right with the world.

The writers of the four Gospels are inseparable. You can't think of one without thinking of the others.

Matthew, Mark, Luke, and John.

TK Clicked for Me

The double-play combination behind me when I was pitching for the San Diego Padres was Templeton to Wiggins to Garvey. It doesn't have quite the right ring, does it?

Garry Templeton, our shortstop, was quite a glove, a talented player who liked to hold the ball while a lumbering catcher huffed and puffed down the first base line only to be beaten by a step from Tempy's lob throw. I'm telling you, he toyed with base runners.

While Garry Templeton was more of a flashy player, I really jelled with a meat-and-potatoes catcher named Terry Kennedy. "TK" is the way I addressed him, and we thought so much alike that it was as if he was talking into an earpiece stuck in my left ear just before I went into my windup.

Thinking alike is really important. Pitchers and catchers are so intertwined—they are called the "battery" in baseball lingo—that if they are not on the same page, then things can quickly go out of kilter on the ball field.

Here's the way it works: the catcher is the one who calls for the pitches (unless the manager or pitching coach is flashing signs from the bench to the catcher). Using his right hand, the catcher crouches behind the plate and flashes a single finger—always the index—when he wants you to throw a fastball. Two fingers—an upside-down "V" sign—is his signal for a deuce, or curveball. Then you have your specialty pitches after that—slider and change-up, signified with three and four fingers. The catcher also points his hand to the inside and outside part of the plate, telling you whether he wants the pitch inside and tight or on the outside corner. If TK wiggled his index finger, that meant he wanted a sinking fastball.

The pitcher has the option of shaking his head no, which is his way of saying, "I don't want to throw a fastball. Give me another sign." And that's when you usually see the deuce go down or a fluttering of all four fingers for a change-up.

Pitchers don't like to stand on the mound with 40,000 in the ballpark and a TV audience watching him shake off signs right and left. It's viewed as being unsure of what pitch to throw, a hesitation that disrupts the rhythm of pitching. In a game where confidence means everything, the seeds of doubt are sewn in the pitcher's mind, and the hitter receives a bit of a confidence boost. That's why a pitcher and a catcher who think alike are a beautiful thing.

Terry Kennedy and I had a beautiful thing going when I pitched to him. We were in sync from the first pitch to the bases-loaded jam with two outs and a 3–2 count. There's something you need to know about pitching: pitchers don't just rear back and throw, they *pitch*. This means they pitch inside with a fastball and come back with a curve on the outside part of the plate. They change speeds and keep the batter guessing and off-balance. Terry and I would get into such a groove that he would flash his sign, and it would be right in line with what I was thinking, and I would go into my windup and fire away. It was as if I could turn off my brain. I was in the zone when I pitched with Terry behind the plate. We had a special relationship that carried off the field, as well.

Bob Knepper, a teammate of mine when I later joined the Giants, told me that one of his regrets was that he was never as tight with any catcher as I was with Terry. His catcher would flash fastball; Bob thought the hitter wouldn't be looking for a curveball. His catcher would signal for a deuce, and Bob was ready to challenge the batter with his best heat. He said there were games where he shook off his catcher fifty times, which is almost half his pitches. All that "shaking off" created an air of indecisiveness on the mound.

There are going to be times when you are indecisive about what to do in life, and it's usually regarding those "gray areas." But God is flashing signs all the time, and they're found in the Bible. Those signs may not be as simple as wig-wagging the index finger or laying down the deuce, but if you spend time in God's Word regularly, you'll come to recognize the signs he's flashing.

The one thing you don't want to do is shake off God. He knows what every hitter is capable of doing against you. No, it's better to go with the pitch he calls.

They Said It

"One's a born liar, and the other's convicted."

—Billy Martin, Yankee manager, commenting on outfielder Reggie Jackson and owner George Steinbrenner, who was convicted for illegal campaign contributions to Richard Nixon's presidential election

PLAYING ON THE "GOD SQUAD"

39

They say that major league ballplayers live in a fishbowl, where every scratch, every spit of tobacco juice, and every twitch are captured by the media. Sounds like a good analogy to me. I have long felt that the media, like fish, need to be fed regularly. Otherwise, they can get on your case, as they do with Barry Bonds, who pretty much disses reporters every chance he gets.

I took a "you win some and you lose some" stance with the media. Some wrote complimentary stories about me that make me blush to this day. Others sharpened their quills and cut me up pretty good.

I guess my low point with the media happened during all the "God Squad" articles that I mentioned a couple chapters ago. If the media has a weakness, it's called writing from the "template." The template for Christian ballplayers is that we are too nice to be winners, that we lack intensity and determination at crunch time, and that when we lose, we shrug our shoulders and mumble, "Praise the Lord."

Most of the time, reporters were careful not to ask me a leading question that I could use as a springboard to talk about my faith. If I talked about baseball, the writers scribbled away furiously, lest one of my words fall harmlessly to the ground. Whenever I mentioned the Lord, however, their pens and pencils stopped moving in unison. Then they looked up to see what I could say next.

I'll never forget the time, though, when the door swung wide open for me to talk about my faith. It happened on a big stage—Game 2 of the 1987 National League Championship Series between the Giants and St. Louis Cardinals. It was a road game at Busch Stadium, and

Roger Craig, our manager, gave me the ball and told me go get those Redbirds.

I responded with probably my best pitching effort ever in a big game: I spun a two-hit shutout, going the distance and extending my postseason record to nineteen and two-thirds innings of shutout ball. I was in the record books.

The media was all over me after the game. This was the playoffs, of course, which drove the coverage. I was led to a media room next to the locker room, where Roger Craig was answering questions. He looked up and saw me as I entered the media room. "They say Christians don't have any guts. Well, this guy's a Christian, and he's not afraid of anything." With that introduction, I sat down in front of a microphone and waited for media to pepper me with questions.

It didn't surprise me when one of the writers played off what my skipper had said. "Roger just commented about what some people say, that Christian athletes don't have guts. How do you respond to that?"

Oh, I loved that question. The writer was basically asking me if Christians were wimps between the lines. "If Jesus was in my shoes and playing Major League baseball, he would be the best athlete on the field," I said. "He would play with more intensity and aggressiveness than any other athlete. But he would always be in control."

The scribes nodded their heads wisely, but I didn't receive any follow-up questions, which is too bad because I would have explained that I was not suggesting that I pictured Jesus as a baseball player. He certainly had more important things to do than to work on his two-seam fastball or hitting with power to the opposite field. But from my reading of the Gospels, everything Jesus did—from preaching to thousands or caring for a single, insignificant person like the woman at the well, he did uncompromisingly, intensely, and powerfully. Jesus was no wimp—far from it. I can easily imagine him playing hard if he were a major league ball player.

What about you? Are you aggressive on the baseball diamond? You should be. When you play baseball, play to glorify God. I don't care how old you are or what level of ball you play at, you want to play to win—not wimp out.

There's another thing you should keep in mind, and it relates to what Byron Ballard (who led me to Christ when I was pitching in the minors) once told me: "Dave, you should pitch as though Jesus Christ is your only audience."

That was a great word picture for me. When I saw Jesus Christ as my only audience, I noticed that the pressure to perform shifted dramatically off my shoulders. That's because I wanted to do my best to bring glory to God, not myself. Sure, any time I pitched poorly stung, but I could walk off the mound knowing that God would always be there for me.

Easier said than done, of course. I needed that reminder of who I was pitching for during perhaps the most critical moment in my career. I had just been called up by the Padres during the 1982 season, and as soon as I arrived in the San Diego clubhouse, I felt the pressure to pitch well, even though I wasn't aware that the Padres were giving me a ten-game trial. That happens in the major leagues, you know. Ball clubs call up players from their AAA team for a mini-tryout all the time. If you don't perform well in the two or three shots you get, you'd get shipped back. It's about as personal as a bank transaction.

Of course, I didn't want to go back, even to a nice place like Hawaii, where I played for the Padres Triple A club. My world was wrapped up with staying *in* the major leagues. I wouldn't say that you're nothing playing in the minors, but you certainly aren't getting candy bars named after you or seeing yourself on *SportsCenter*.

Early in my trial period, I'll never forget the pit in my stomach during a Saturday Game of the Week played under the sunlight of Candlestick Park. I knew the TV cameras were everywhere, which made me more nervous by the minute.

I was shaking like a leaf when I got called into the game. Two men on, left-handed hitter at the plate, game on the line. I was the setup reliever: my job was to get the left-handed hitter out and give way to someone like Goose Gossage to finish the Giants off.

My job was not to walk the batter, but that's what I did—a total choke job. I was a control pitcher; that was my bread and butter. I didn't blow hitters away like Randy Johnson. Instead, I used pinpoint control to keep hitters off balance and swinging at my pitches.

My pitching coach, Norm Sherry, dropped by my locker after the game. I was slumped over, staring ahead. "You've got to throw strikes, Dave, or they're going to send you back to Hawaii," he said as he gave me a pat on the back.

The next day, I received a phone call from Mark Thurmond, one of my teammates with the Padres' Triple A team in Honolulu. He had seen me pitch on national TV, and he was appalled. He told me that I pitched as if I was stepping on eggshells each time I planted my front foot. "Dave, don't you remember anything?" he said. "Are you forgetting what got you there? Be a tiger! Don't nibble at these guys. Go after them!"

I mumbled my thanks, but I couldn't admit to Mark that I was scared to be standing on a big league mound with 40,000 people in the park, watching my every move.

The next day, the team flew to Los Angeles, where Jan and Tiffany drove up to meet me at the team hotel. Jan, who knew the moods of her husband, saw the black clouds following me around like a street urchin.

"What's wrong, sweetie? I know something's wrong."

I told her that if I didn't start throwing strikes real soon, we would be working on our tans in Honolulu again. That may sound like a problem millions of couples would love to have, but for Jan and me, going back to Hawaii would have been a demotion. And once demoted from The Show, it's hard to get a return ticket. "Norm says that's why they brought me up, because I knew how to get the ball over the plate. But I'm not doing it."

"Why can't you throw strikes?" Jan asked, as if it was the easiest thing in the world for me to do.

"I'm scared, Jan." And then I started crying. Jan never saw me crying. To cry was to admit weakness, but when Jan saw the tears in my eyes, her eyes flooded. We held each other close and let it go.

"There's nothing to be afraid of," she said after the longest moment. "All you can do is your best. If that's not good enough for them, so what? What's the worst thing that could happen? We get sent back to Hawaii. I'd love to go back. I liked it better there. We'd see our friends again."

Then it hit me. If I failed, it didn't matter to Jan. If I failed, it didn't matter to my audience of one—Jesus Christ. He still loved me, just as Jan loved me. Their love wasn't conditional.

That night, I was called in for another relief stint. This time as I stood on the mound at Chavez Ravine, I took a deep breath and reminded myself that Jesus was my only audience. I was playing for him, and to a lesser extent, my family. I was in a win-win situation. I started getting a few batters out, and then Ron Cey, "The Penguin," stepped into the batter's box with a man on first.

Cey ripped one into the alley, but left fielder Gene Richards couldn't glove it. He smashed into the Dodger blue fence head-on, so he was taken out of the play. While the ball caromed off the wall, the footrace was on. Bill Russell, the runner, scored standing up, and the third-base coach was waving Cey in for an inside-the-park home run.

The relay throw had Cey beat by a mile, but the ball bounced over Terry Kennedy's head. I was alertly (ha!) backing up the play. I pounced on the ball, whirled, and threw a strike to Kennedy, who slapped a tag on the sliding Penguin.

"Yer out!" the umpire bellowed.

That was the only run I gave up. The bang-bang play at the plate energized me, and the next night, I *wanted* to pitch. Manager

Dick Williams must have seen some spark in my eyes, so he gave me the ball again. This time I responded with three innings of shut-out ball, and I never looked back. I could throw strikes, and my stuff could get major league hitters out.

That lesson has stayed with me. Today, I no longer pitch as if Jesus were my only audience, but I certainly try to live like he is the only one in the stands.

They Said It

Mickey Mantle: (pointing at a Jolly Roger pirate flag flying from the mast of a make-believe pirate ship): "I bet you don't know what the skull and crossbones on that flag means."

Yogi Berra: "Sure I do. It means iodine."

THE BIBLE OF BASEBALL 40

You know the Bible is full of baseball, don't you?

You say you weren't aware of that? Well, you only have to look at the very first sentence of Scripture to read where baseball was first mentioned in the Bible. In Genesis 1:1, we learn that in the big inning, God created the heavens and the earth.

Yuck, yuck, yuck, yuck. God must have had a long at bat when he created the heavens and the earth. But did you know that after the big inning, Eve stole first, Adam stole second, and the prodigal son ran home?

I know—I should have been a stand-up comic instead of a baseball pitcher. Like Samson, I would have brought the house down.

Stop, Dave, you're killing me!

I know. These jokes were old when Abner Doubleday was young. But sometimes when I read my Bible, I can't help but see some names that I've seen before—like Hank Aaron and Babe Ruth, if you catch my drift.

So I did a little research, and I found the major leagues have been peopled by hundreds of players whose first or last names have appeared in the Bible. Take *Adam,* for instance. Sixteen major league players have had the first name Adam, and interestingly, that name must be enjoying a renaissance because six of those are playing today, including Adam Eaton, a Padre pitcher. I didn't find any players named *Eve,* although Ever Magallanes (1991) came close. Johnny Evers, the midpoint of the famous "Tinker to Evers to Chance" double-play team of the 1910s with the Chicago Cubs, deserves an honorable mention.

The Old Testament is full of baseball players:

- Shawn *Abner* (1987–92) played five years with the Padres. He's one of three little Abners.
- *Asa* Brainard (1871–74) and *Asa* Stratton (1881) played in the nineteenth century, and yes, they were guys.
- I mentioned the great Hank *Aaron,* but there are close to ten players with *Aaron* as their first name in the big leagues today. Aaron Boone is a third-generation ballplayer: his father, Bob, and grandfather, Ray, were impact players in their day.
- Three *Cains* made it to the majors, including Sugar *Cain* (1932–38). *Abel* Lizotte (1896) batted .103 in seven games.

- *Caleb* Johnson didn't get a chance to spy on other teams; he played in just sixteen games in 1871.
- *Eli* Marrero, a Cuban player, has played for St. Louis since 1997. He is one of four *Eli* players in major league history.
- *Elijah* Jones was a September call-up for the Detroit Tigers at the end of the 1907 and 1909 seasons. The biblical Elijah called on God to rain down fire on his sacrifice to prove that the prophets of Baal didn't have what it takes to stay in the game.
- *Ezra* Lincoln (1890), *Ezra* Midkiff (1909–1913), and *Ezra* Sutton (1871–88) made it to the big leagues. Ezra, a scribe among the exiles in Babylon, led 2,000 men and their families back to the major league city for Jews—Jerusalem.
- Brett *Gideon* (1987–90) and Jim *Gideon* (1975) saw a few Gideon Bibles when they traveled.
- I wonder how Truck *Hannah* (1918–20) got his first name.
- I wonder how *Hezekiah* Allen (1884) got *his* first name.
- Nine players with the last name Jacobs made it to the big leagues, but *Jacob* Cruz (1996–present) is one of two Jacob players. He's still playing today. And then you have Jacobs Field, home of the Cleveland Indians.
- *Jeremiah* Reardon (1886) pitched only ten innings in major league baseball and had an ERA of 9.0.
- Von *Joshua* (1969–80) was a good player, playing ten seasons with a career batting average of .273.
- *Mordecai* "Three Fingers" Brown (1903–16) lost parts of fingers in a farming accident as a young boy, but he still developed "the best curveball in the game," according to Ty Cobb. Mordecai, who threw with parts of three fingers and his thumb, was inducted into the Baseball Hall of Fame in 1949.
- Wally *Moses* (1935–51) played seventeen seasons, but he could never lead his team to the Promised Land of the World Series.

- I think I could have been friends with Joe *Nathan* (1999–present), who pitches for the Giants today. Nathan was a great friend and advisor of David.
- The best head count I can give you on *David* is . . . wait a minute, we're talking about me—*Dave* Dravecky!
- *Reuben* Ewing (1921) batted once in the big leagues, striking out.
- *Samuel Jethroe* (1950–54) sounds like he played for the Jerusalem Giants.
- *Saul* Rogovin (1949–57) was responsible for the Chicago White Sox pennant run in 1951.
- I wonder how smart a player Eddie *Solomon* (1973–82) was when he played.

For New Testament players:

- *Joseph* has had a great career, including the Yankee Clipper, Joe DiMaggio, and several hundred other Joes.
- Hallelujah! *Luke* Easter, a black player who must have thought his chances to play were dead, saw his career resurrected in 1949 when he signed with the Cleveland Indians.
- *Matt Luke* (1996–99) was born Matthew Clifford Luke, not Matthew Mark Luke.
- I didn't have time to count how many *Johns* we've had in the majors, but Tommy *John* (1963–89) had a surgery named after him. Tommy was diagnosed with a career-threatening torn ulnar collateral ligament in 1974. Dr. Frank Jobe (pronounced like *Job* of the Old Testament) made history when he extracted a tendon from Tommy's right arm and used it to replace the torn ligament on his left, pitching arm, threading the healthy tendon through holes drilled into the bone above and below the elbow.
- Only one player has gone by Philip—*Philip* Nastu (1978–80), a Giant pitcher who preceded me by about ten years. I

can think of many Phils, though, like Hall of Famer *Phil* Niekro (1964–87) and current Padre *Phil* Nevin.

- I've never doubted the talent of Frank *Thomas* (1990–present), but the Big Hurt has been a Big Headache for the Chicago White Sox, distancing himself from teammates with extended clubhouse pouts and occasional late arrivals.

"I know the name, but I can't replace the face."

—Johnny Logan, Milwaukee Braves shortstop

AN ANGEL ON THE MOUND 41

Sometimes late at night, when I think of what might have been following the amputation of my left arm, I wonder if I could have become a major league pitcher if I had lost my *right* arm as a young kid. Could I have become an effective pitcher firing away with a single limb? Would I have been able to generate enough heat to keep the batters at bay?

The answer is a flat-out no. There's no way on earth that a one-armed pitcher—and I'm talking about someone whose arm has been amputated at the shoulder—could generate a motion that would allow him to pitch a ball to the plate with major league gas. In ways that you would never think, you need both arms to give you balance as you wind up, coil, and release the pitch toward the plate. Pitching with one arm would be like downhill skiing with one arm: it can be done, but only at the amateur level. The other thing is that you couldn't wear a mitt, so you'd be fielding your position barehanded.

Now, if you know your baseball, you may be wondering: *What about Jim Abbott? Didn't he have one arm?*

You would be referring to Jim Abbott, who pitched for the California Angels, New York Yankees, Chicago White Sox, and the Milwaukee Brewers during the 1990s. Actually, Jim was born with one *hand,* which makes a difference, as I just explained. I'll have more to say about that, but for now, let me tell you more about this remarkable pitcher who broke in with the California Angels in 1989—which, coincidentally, was my "comeback" year with the San Francisco Giants. Since Jim was playing in the American League, however, our paths never crossed because interleague ball hadn't started yet. But I remember all the hoopla surrounding his rookie season.

I first heard about Jim when he became the first baseball player to win the Sullivan Award in 1987, an honor given to the nation's top amateur athlete. Following a standout career at the University of Michigan, Jim pitched for the U.S. Olympic baseball team that captured the gold medal at the 1988 Summer Games in Seoul, South Korea. After being picked in the first round of the major league draft by the California Angels, he pitched his way into the Angel starting rotation during spring training in 1989, thus making the rare jump from college baseball to the major leagues without ever spending a day in the minors.

Jim received a ton of great publicity that spring. Since I was recuperating from major surgery (doctors had excised much of the deltoid muscle in my left arm in an attempt to rid my body of cancer), I had time on my hands to thumb through lengthy features in *Time, Newsweek,* and *Sports Illustrated* devoted to Jim's overnight ascent to the majors. *Life* magazine even presented one of their famous "Day in the Life" photo spreads with full-sized shots of Jim strolling along the beach in Southern California. *Baseball America* breathlessly announced that only Jackie Robinson breaking the color barrier in 1947 topped Jim's rookie debut.

Jim said that he received hundreds of letters from handicapped children and parents of handicapped youngsters congratulating him for making it to the big leagues. I think I know how Jim felt because I was bowled over by the letters I received from thousands of cancer survivors wishing me the best.

I followed Jim's progress during his rookie season, and he performed well, winning twelve games (against twelve losses) while handcuffing hitters with a cut fastball. He became one of only three pitchers during the 1980s to win his first professional game at the major league level.

After his excellent debut, Jim went on to fashion a fine ten-year career that brought him incredible highs (an eighteen-game winning season in 1991 and throwing a no-hitter in Yankee pinstripes in 1993) and incredible lows (a disastrous 2–18 season in 1996 with the Angels and his outright release).

Now let's return to our previous discussion about one-armed pitchers. As I mentioned before, Jim was a *one-handed* pitcher because he was born with a normal left arm and a right arm that extended to his wrist. No one understood why he was born that way, but it happened. His parents fitted him with a prosthetic hand with a hook when he was four years old, but he hated the hook look, especially after being on the receiving end of mean teasing from other kids. After a year of wearing the hook, Jim's parents let him stash it in the closet.

Jim says his father encouraged him to be outgoing and not ashamed of his disability. If Jim met someone he didn't know, he extended his left hand and said, "Hi, I'm Jim Abbott." This taught the young boy not to hang back in the shadows of life but to feel that he had a place, that he was *normal*.

Jim loved to run, play sports, and do everything else his friends did. No one batted an eye when he declared that he wanted to play Little League baseball. The young boy developed a clever way to overcome the lack of a right hand. With the ball placed in a right-handed glove, he rested the back of his mitt against his chest by cradling it with his right arm. Then he reached for the ball with his left hand, slid the glove to the tip of the right stub, inserted the stub into the glove pocket, went into his windup, and delivered his pitch. Before you could say "Jack Robinson," he slipped his left hand into the glove so that he would be ready to field his position. If he had to field a batted ball, he would transfer the ball into his left hand in a split second and make the throw to first base. If the catcher tossed the ball back to him following the pitch, he caught the ball with his left hand, and then cradled the mitt to his chest in one smooth motion so that he could grab the ball to start his windup. Jim developed this unique talent by devoting hours and hours throwing a rubber ball against a brick wall.

A *one-armed* pitcher wouldn't have the luxury of being able to cradle a mitt against his chest. I would have been a defensive liability on the field, since I would have to play my position without a glove. I tell you this, though: I would have barehanded any hot liner back to the box or taken a shot into the gut, if that's what it took to get into the game. But as I said before, I believe a pitcher would need a portion of his non-throwing arm to:

- make a motion that could help him throw the ball fast
- use a glove in the same manner as Jim did so that he could field his position

When Jim pitched in high school ball, opposing coaches thought they could bunt on him. One team had eight hitters in a row bunt against him, even though Jim threw out the last seven. For all the success Jim had in fielding bunts, however, I still think a one-armed pitcher is vulnerable to the bunt.

But you know what? I think Jim did something even more amazing than pitching that no-hit game for the Yankees. In 1999, Jim became the only other person besides Pete Gray—the one-armed outfielder for the St. Louis Browns during the 1945 season—to stroke a hit against major league pitching while holding the bat with one hand. (You'll learn more about Pete Gray in our next chapter.)

Here's how that happened. Jim's final stop in the big leagues found him in Milwaukee, where he played for the Brewers. Up until then, Jim had pitched in the American League, where the designated hitter took the pitcher's place in the batting lineup. In the National League, however, pitchers always bat number nine in the batting order. I had enjoyed taking my hacks when I was playing, but with a lifetime average of a buck twenty-five (.125), I'm glad that I didn't have to rely on hitting skills to keep me in the majors. Otherwise, I would have been looking for another line of work very quickly.

If you will indulge me, I must relate my biggest moment as a batter. It happened in San Diego when I jacked a Dennis Powell fastball over the fence for my one and only major league home run. I rounded the bases with a huge grin, but that grin turned to a frown when it became apparent that I provided the only offense that day: the Padres lost 2–1 to the Los Angeles Dodgers.

Jim Abbott generated some offense as well during his one season in the National League. Jim stroked two singles in 21 at bats while assuming a batting stance that had him swinging with one hand. That feat astounds me because the last time Jim stepped into the batter's box against live pitching was fifteen years previously on his high school baseball team in Flint, Michigan. Maybe I shouldn't be so astounded because Jim batted .433 in high school and hit six home runs—one-handed. But this time around, he was facing major league pitching.

Jim was a remarkable athlete who overcame tremendous odds, skeptical coaches, and his own disability to make it to the upper reaches of the great game of baseball. I salute him for what he accomplished from the pitcher's mound—and from the batting box.

They Said It

"We didn't form the basis for a major league career. We just played catch."

—Jim Abbott, when asked what his father did to prepare him for a major league pitching career.

"I wanted to be like Nolan Ryan. I didn't want to be like Pete Gray."

—Jim Abbott, pitcher

PETE GRAY:
THE ONE-ARMED WONDER

42

While the story of Jim Abbott is extraordinary, you're going to find the story of Pete Gray even more astonishing. It's one thing to pitch with one arm—it's quite another to make your living batting with one arm.

Perhaps you've never heard of Pete Gray, which is understandable because he played more than fifty years ago for the St. Louis Browns at the end of World War II. As the only position player to reach the major leagues with one arm, Pete played in the majors for a lot longer than a cup of coffee—77 games during his one season in the bigs. You may ask, *How was that possible?*

The answer lies in the era he played in. Pete was born in 1915 in Nanticoke, Pennsylvania, and that's where he died eighty-seven years later in 2002. Perhaps you remember reading his obituary, but you need more than a few sentences to describe what this man accomplished on the baseball diamond.

Pete was just a six-year-old kid who liked to play baseball in vacant lots when his life took a dramatic turn. One day, he was riding on the running board of a truck, probably a Ford Model A, when he slipped. His right arm got caught up in one of the wheels. The horrible accident mangled his right arm—his throwing arm.

Doctors could not save the boy's arm, so they amputated it at the shoulder. They didn't take part of the shoulder, however, as they had done with me. I can only imagine the emotional trauma that the young boy experienced in losing a limb, and I'm sure he experienced despair and resignation. Eventually, Pete went on with life, and like any youngster growing up in the 1920s, he wanted to play baseball with his friends. He taught himself to throw left-handed, and a cobbler in Nanticoke stitched up a custom glove for him. The glove, which was smaller than usual, had most of the padding removed.

This way he could shake the glove off quickly to field a slow-rolling ball in the outfield (Pete would have been a liability in the infield), or slide the glove fully onto his hand when a line drive or fly ball came his way. He became very proficient at catching the ball, tucking the thin glove under his stump, taking the ball out with his left hand, rolling it across his chest to get a grip on it, and throwing it back to the infield. With practice, he could perform all these moves in one fluid motion.

But what about hitting? Pete held the bat with his left hand and swung one-handed. Let me say something about that. After my arm was amputated, I missed playing one of my favorite sports—golf. But you can hit a golf ball with one arm! Instructors will sometimes ask right-handed players to swing with the left arm only to get used to how much the left arm comes into play on a natural swing. Since I had only a right arm and played right-handed, that wasn't going to help me. Still, with practice, I managed to learn how to hit a golf ball with just my right arm, and I'm proud to say that I boom some drives 240 to 250 yards off the tee! (Oh, by the way, I live in Colorado at the 7,000-foot level. My foot wedge goes 150 yards.)

Pete Gray wasn't trying to hit a small white ball sitting up on a tee. He was trying to hit a pitch coming at him at 80 or 90 mph and get enough wood on the ball to drive it out of the infield. He used a full-weight, regulation bat, not some lighter model, and grabbed the bat about six inches up from the handle. Then he stepped deep into the batter's box and took a full cut at the pitch. Can you imagine how difficult that might have been to put wood on the horsehide? Try doing that with a whiffle ball or a softball the next time you're swinging a bat!

Pete had excellent hand-eye coordination, and he became an accomplished bunter. How did he bunt? Pete would plant the knob of the bat against the side of his abdomen, and then press the butt of the bat into his body while he slid his hand about a third of the way up the shaft. He had great raw speed, which allowed him to beat out bunts and run like a gazelle on the base paths.

Pete developed into an excellent player, given his disability. Born Peter Wyshner, he changed his name to Pete Gray, probably so he would sound Americanized. He played semipro ball in the coal towns of his native Pennsylvania for a few years before he found a professional team willing to take him on—in Canada. In 1938, Pete joined the Trois Rivieres of the Quebec Provincial League. He acquitted himself well: he batted .283, collecting 17 hits in 60 at-bats. The record shows that he one-handed a home run out of the ballpark, which astounds me. How would you like to have been the pitcher who gave up a gopher ball to a one-armed hitter?

Not much is known about where Pete played from 1939–41, but he popped up again in Quebec when he returned to Trois Rivieres. In 42 games, he hit .381. Then Pete moved up to the Southern Association in 1943, where he batted .289 over a full season with Memphis. The following year was his best yet: he batted .333 for Memphis, hit five home runs, tied a league record by stealing 68 bases (I told you he was fast), and was named the Southern Association's MVP. That won him some national attention—the one-armed player more than holding his own with some of the best minor league players in the country.

Actually, Pete wasn't playing against the best minor leaguers, and here's where the story turns interesting. The nation was at war in the early 1940s, and by 1944, more than half of the major league players were serving in the armed forces. This development presented a window of opportunity for career minor league players such as Pete. The empty seats on major league benches were filled with has-beens and never-weres, plus older players ineligible for the draft.

The St. Louis Browns, a longtime American League doormat, handed Pete a major league uniform at the start of the 1945 season.

He was viewed as a wartime happening, a curious oddity that fit with the mood of a country that had sent millions of troops into harm's way in the European and Pacific theaters. In every city he visited, the baseball writers devoted reams of copy to his remarkable and inspirational story.

It's too bad that many fans and players didn't quite see Pete in the same light. He was taunted everywhere he played, hearing such insults as, "You're never going to make it, crip," and "Wait until the real players come back, cripple." Pete's response was to retreat into a shell, or, to use a wartime description, stay in his bunker and shut out the world. He told interviewers that he kept his own company in those days, which is why he received a reputation for being hard to get along with.

Pete played every other day and got into exactly half of the St. Louis Browns' games. He stepped up to the plate 234 times and one-armed 51 hits for a .218 average in 77 games. I would say that was excellent hitting—better than many of today's shortstops—and I don't care if the quality of Major League Baseball *was* at an all-time low. His batting average would have been higher if outfielders had played him at normal depth, but they moved *way* in and caught many of his Texas Leaguers in the air, robbing him of a single. Pete couldn't hit for power, and everyone in the ballpark knew it.

His best game came at Yankee Stadium—a doubleheader at the House That Ruth Built. Pete banged out four hits, scored twice, drove in two runs, made three outstanding catches, handled nine chances in the field cleanly, and scored the winning run as the Browns swept the depleted Yanks on May 20, 1945. Okay, so these weren't the Bronx Bombers of yesteryear, but it was still major league ball on the game's greatest stage.

When World War II ended with the Allies' victory in the summer of 1945, Pete's days as a Major League player were numbered. The Browns sent Pete down at the 1946 spring training camp, but he continued to play minor league ball and barnstorm until the early 1950s. People wanted to see the one-armed player who made it to the major leagues. When his baseball days were over, Pete returned to Nanticoke, Pennsylvania, where it's said that he became a recluse until his death. Today, you can see his hand-stitched baseball glove in the Baseball Hall of Fame in Cooperstown, New York.

Pete played baseball long before the Americans with Disabilities Act became the law of the land and long before disabled activists spoke out for equal treatment. I've often wondered why people insult others because of a physical disability. Pete slipped off a running board as a young child, and in an instant of horror, his right arm was chewed up in wheel spokes. Don't people understand that he didn't mean to slip—that it was an accident? Do they think that the child *wanted* his arm amputated?

It's an old saying that you don't appreciate something until you don't have it any longer. I certainly took my left arm for granted for more than thirty years, and then I lost it. I often said that I felt as if I lost a lifelong, dear friend. So, dear reader, if you have all your limbs, all your extremities, then you have much to be thankful for. If you have your eyesight and good hearing, you have much to be thankful for. If you can get out of a La-Z-Boy and walk to the refrigerator, you have much to be thankful for.

When's the last time you thanked God for your good health and a complete body? Maybe today would be a good time to praise him and express your appreciation for health that's easy to take for granted.

Meet the One-Arm Bandits

Pete Gray might not have been the inspiration behind Jim Abbott, but he was certainly the inspiration behind the formation of a softball team made up of mostly one-arm players. The One-Arm Bandits, who are from Miami-Dade County in South Florida, are a softball team in which fifteen of the eighteen players are missing an arm or part of an arm. Some players lost their arms in tragic accidents; others, like team founder Victor Rosario, were simply born with one arm. They compete in a C division fast-pitch softball league comprised of full-bodied players.

The one-armed players bat with one arm, just like Pete Gray did, but unlike Pete, they swing lighter bats. Most use twenty-three-ounce bats, several ounces lighter than regular softball bats. Since some play infield positions, they field ground balls a little differently. They field the grounder with their gloved hand, drop the glove like a hot potato, grab the ball out of the glove, and throw to first base. The able-bodied players play shortstop, center field, and pitch.

The team traveled to Venezuela to play a five-game series against the newly formed Bandidos de un Solo Brazo (that would be One-Arm Bandits in Spanish) in the first international game in the history of softball in which two one-arm teams competed against each other. The goodwill games were televised throughout Venezuela and drew crowds of over 2,000 spectators. Team members visited Venezuelan children's hospitals to offer encouragement to those suffering the trauma of a sudden amputation. "God didn't give us all the limbs you need to play baseball," said Victor Rosario, "but maybe that's why he gave us a little bit more heart."

Someone told Pete about the One-Arm Bandits before his death, and relatives said he was pleased and touched that he was their spiritual hero. Victor wanted to take the team to Pete's hometown in Nanticoke, Pennsylvania, so that he could see the team in action, but it never worked out, although he did send Victor a signed picture.

Victor told me that he shows Pete's autographed picture to teams and children that they touch along the way, which somehow seems fitting. But let me tell you, these One-Arm Bandits are an inspiration to me.

They Said It

"Pete Gray shows us something every day. You really don't believe some of the things he does. Believe me, he can show plenty of two-handed outfielders plenty."

—Luke Sewell, St. Louis Browns manager in 1945

WARTIME BASEBALL

43

You only have to look at the Iraqi war and World War II as a reminder of how much the world has changed. Sixty years ago, this nation mobilized for war following the attack on Pearl Harbor, and it took more than three years to defeat the Axis powers—Germany, Japan, and Italy. The Iraqi war that destroyed Saddam Hussein's brutal regime basically took three weeks. We watched the liberation of Iraq unfold in real time as it happened on CNN and Fox News, but back in World War II, Americans received their war news by watching newsreels weeks after the battle.

There are other differences. In the 1940s, a military draft of able-bodied males provided the manpower for the armed services, and baseball's biggest names served our country. Today, we have an all-volunteer force, and nobody expects Alex Rodriguez to set aside his $22,000,000 a year salary to play Army baseball for several hundred bucks a month and all the MREs he can eat.

In the 1940s, baseball was the only game on the block—the National Pastime that captured the hearts and imagination of a nation. Today, baseball fights for attention against NFL football, college football, NBA basketball, March Madness, NHL hockey, NASCAR racing, and a dozen other athletic endeavors that range from tennis and golf (the Williams sisters and Tiger Woods) to "extreme" sports like snowboarding and skateboard luge (the X Games).

Shortly after the nation was shocked by the Japanese sneak attack on Pearl Harbor on December 7, 1941—a date that will "live in infamy," said President Franklin D. Roosevelt—baseball owners wondered if they should continue to "play ball" for the "duration." Nobody knew in those early, dark days, how long the war would last. To seek clarification on where baseball stood, commissioner Kenesaw Mountain Landis wrote President Franklin D. Roosevelt regarding that question and received this reply:

Honorable Kenesaw M. Landis
333 North Michigan Avenue
Chicago, Illinois
January 15, 1942

My Dear Judge,

Thank you for yours of January fourteenth. As you will, of course, realize the final decision about the baseball season must rest with you and the baseball club owners—so what I am going to say is solely a personal and not an official point of view.

I honestly feel that it would be best for the country to keep baseball going. There will be fewer people unemployed, and everybody will work longer hours and harder than ever before. And that means that they ought to have a chance for recreation and taking their minds off their work even more than before.

Baseball provides a recreation which does not last two hours or two hours and a half, and which can be gotten for very little cost. And, incidentally, I hope that night games can be extended because it gives an opportunity to the day shift to see a game occasionally.

As to the players themselves, I know you agree with me that individual players who are of military or naval age should go, without question, into the services. Even if the actual quality to the teams is lowered by the greater use of older players, this will not dampen the popularity of the sport. Of course, if an individual has some particular aptitude in a trade or a profession, he ought to serve the Government. That, however, is a matter which I know you can handle with complete justice.

Here is another way of looking at it: if 300 teams use 5,000 or 6,000 players, these players are a definite recreational asset to at least 20,000,000 of their fellow citizens, and that in my judgment is thoroughly worthwhile.

> With every best wish,
> Very sincerely yours,
> (signed) Franklin Delano Roosevelt
> The White House
> Washington

Several items are noteworthy in FDR's letter, and it's not the lack of zip codes. First, the President answered Commissioner Landis one day after he received the letter, which tells you how important that issue was to him. Second, FDR said, "Hey, it's basically up to you, but if I were you, I'd keep playing." And third, it sure sounds as if FDR expected *everyone* of military age to serve in the armed forces.

Just about every major league ballplayer *did* serve, although it's a mind-blower to learn that 95 percent of Major League players—some 565 in all—swapped cleats for combat boots during World War II. Most players did not have to be pressured into the enlistment office, although some like Ted Williams and Joe DiMaggio sought deferments in 1942 and played that season. Public sentiment was such, however, that Williams and DiMaggio quickly enlisted after the '42 season; to not serve would risk being called a "slacker." Many of the stars who did enlist, like DiMaggio, were treated with kid gloves and given "important" jobs, like playing baseball for touring service teams that entertained the troops. Others like Ted Williams, however, became pilots who flew on missions and lived to see another day.

Baseball was seen as a unifying force in World War II. Jack Lait, a writer with the *New York Mirror,* probably said it best when he wrote about the meaning of baseball to America. "Today, the whack of the bat, the ballyhoo of the hot dog and ice cream cone boys, the hoarse commands of the umpires and the shrieks of the frantic fans blend into a symphony of liberty, of independence, and of Americanism," he wrote in the early days of World War II. "God has blessed America in many ways, and happily, baseball is one of his numerous manifestations. To citizens in mufti and to young men in khaki, it offers a common meeting place, where freedom of expression is unfettered, class distinctions are leveled, and rivalries can be settled without bloodshed or slaughter of innocents."

That was well said, but World War II did some strange things to the grand old game. Baseballs were made with a hard plastic core to conserve rubber, but the ball didn't travel as far. Teams didn't go to Florida for spring training because of wartime travel restrictions; instead they conducted "spring" training on muddy, snow-ringed fields outside New York, Boston, and Philadelphia. Night games in New York and Boston were scratched because of blackout restrictions; authorities believed that the cities were vulnerable to a German submarine attack.

When the games were played, it was evident that the talent pool had dipped considerably. Hank Greenberg, baseball's first Jewish star and the first player to take a serious run at Babe Ruth's home record with 58 home runs in 1938, estimated that the war reduced the level of Major League Baseball by 25 percent. That's a low estimate, given that nearly every able-bodied major league player was off to war. Teams restocked their lineups with bush leaguers who would have never gotten near a major league tryout, let alone play in the vast expanses of Yankee Stadium and Fenway Park.

I've already talked about players like Pete Gray, the one-armed outfielder, donning the flannel uniform of the St. Louis Browns during the 1945 season. Pete, however, wasn't the only physically handicapped player during wartime:

- Paul O'Dea played with one eye for the Cleveland Indians.
- Dick Sipek couldn't hear; he played for the Cincinnati Reds.
- Whitey Kurowski, a third baseman for the St. Louis Cardinals, threw with an arm six inches shorter than the other.

Although World War II ended in the spring and summer of 1945, major league servicemen didn't return stateside until late in the year. When spring training camps opened in 1946, teams were flooded with prewar stars and players anxious to resume their major league careers. Some, like Joe DiMaggio and Ted Williams, didn't miss a beat. Others noticed that they had lost a step in the outfield or a foot on their fastball. Many pitchers worked on their breaking stuff that spring, hoping to win back a spot in the rotation with off-speed pitching.

Some players couldn't come back, which I can identify with. Cecil Travis, a Washington Senators shortstop, suffered frozen feet during the famous Battle of the Bulge in late 1944. Skippy Roberge, a Boston Braves infielder, and Lou Thuman, a Senators pitcher, got shot up. But at least they came back in one piece and not in a pine box.

One minor league player didn't come back in one piece. Bert Shepard, a journeyman pitcher, had his right leg amputated just below the knee after his fighter plane crashed in Germany. How Bert got to the major leagues *after* his amputation is a remarkable story. It begins in 1937, when he was seventeen years old. Bert and a friend rode the rails from his Indiana home to Southern California in search of adventure. He worked in a tire retread plant while pitching for every sandlot baseball team who'd take him. A Chicago White Sox scout spotted him, signed him to a sixty-dollars-a-month contract, and shipped him to Longview, Texas, where he promptly blew his arm out trying to impress White Sox coaches.

In 1940, Bert caught on with a minor league team in Wisconsin Rapids, but he was a wild pitcher. He bounced around the minors until his draft number came up in May 1942. Then it was off to boot camp at Daniel Field near Augusta, Georgia, where Bert surprised himself by applying for pilot training. He had never flown in an airplane before.

Bert showed good aptitude to flying, and he was trained to fly a P–38 fighter aircraft. After six weeks of training, he was stationed with the 55th Fighter Group of the U.S. 8th Air Force, based in Scotland. By the spring of 1944, he had participated in more than two dozen missions, mainly over Berlin.

May 21, 1944 turned out to be a fateful day in Bert's life. Though he wasn't scheduled to fly that day, he volunteered to join a massive air strike on Berlin. His orders were to strafe and bomb an aerodrome.

About a mile from the field, German artillery fire intensified. Bert was hit, and when he looked down, his right foot was gone. Bert also took a nick in the chin, causing him to slump forward. *Mayday, mayday!* He crash-landed as his P–38 exploded into flames.

The American pilot doesn't know how he escaped the flaming wreckage, but his first memory was waking up in a German field hospital several days later, terribly banged up. The right leg from the ankle on down was gone.

When he had sufficiently recovered from his injuries, Bert was shipped off to a prisoner-of-war camp. Don't ask me how this was possible, but a fellow prisoner made a crude artificial leg out of scrap metal for Bert. There wasn't much to do but play catch in Stalag 9-C.

He caught a break when his name came up in trade talks between the Germans and Americans. He was exchanged for a German prisoner and shipped back to New York harbor in February 1945. He soon received a new artificial leg. While in New York, he was introduced to Secretary of War Robert Patterson. As they made small talk, Bert mentioned that he wanted to give professional baseball a try. When the Secretary mentioned that he might have a problem doing it on one good leg, Bert replied that he would try anyway.

The next time Secretary Patterson was in Washington, he telephoned Clark Griffith, owner of the American League Washington Nationals, and told him about the one-legged prisoner of war looking to play professional baseball. With the 1945 season right around the corner, Griffith said he'd give the young pitcher a look-over. Griffith figured that at the worst, he and the team would receive some good publicity for giving a disabled war hero a shot at his dreams.

Many observers couldn't tell that Bert Shepard pitched with an artificial leg because he walked so well on it. As a left-handed pitcher, he was fortunate, if that would be the right word, that he lost his right foot since he pushed off the mound with his back or left foot. Otherwise, he never could have pitched with any velocity. With a good foot to throw off, Bert generated a pretty good fastball. At spring training that year, reporters and photographers flocked to do a story on the twenty-four-year-old war veteran trying to make the Washington Nationals with one leg. He was portrayed as a symbol of courage in American young people—The War Hero Pitcher.

The Nationals felt, however, that they couldn't commit a roster spot to an untested rookie amputee pitcher, so they offered Bert a coaching contract and had him pitch batting practice. He pitched in some exhibition games and more than held his own. Although it didn't look as though he'd get a chance to play in the regular season, he still had a great view from the bench.

One time in Boston, Bert was pitching batting practice again. He tossed a few pitches when he heard a cracking sound. It was his wooden leg, starting to show signs of cracking. He brushed it off, then went into his windup, and this time the leg turned sideways. Again, he brushed it off, and during his next windup, he brought his leg up, kicked, and watched in horror as his right shoe and foot flew on a line toward center field. Early bird fans at Fenway Park nearly fainted in shock, and Bert's fellow ballplayers doubled over in laughter.

In the middle of the season, Bert pitched in another exhibition game, this one against the Brooklyn Dodgers, which was billed as a war relief fund-raiser. He acquitted himself well, giving up two runs in a 3–2 victory. He got the win.

His fine performance won him a roster spot. Now he was an active player, but the Nationals were deep into a pennant race, so he was told not to get his hopes up. On August 4, 1945, however, the Boston Red Sox had scored twelve runs in the top of the fourth inning in the second game of a doubleheader. Why waste a good arm and two good legs on a blowout?

Bert Shepard received the phone call in the Nats' pen to start warming up. A few minutes later, he walked, if a bit stiff-legged, to the mound. He had inherited a bases-loaded jam, two outs, with George "Catfish" Metkovich pawing the dirt. On a 3–2 count, Bert reeled in Catfish with a waist-high fastball that the batter swung at and missed.

Bert kept pitching—the fifth, the sixth, the seventh, the eighth, and the ninth innings. He limited the Red Sox to one run on three hits. That turned out to be the only time that Bert's name became part of a major league box score. The veterans were coming back for the 1946 season, so Bert cashed in on his celebrity and joined barnstorming teams. He bounced around the minor leagues before calling it a career in 1955.

Bert is still alive, living his golden years with his wife, Betty, in Hesperia, California. He's a great golfer, having once played to a four handicap. He won the National Amputee Golf Tournament twice when he was in his late forties and early fifties.

Players like Bert Shepard, Pete Gray, and Jim Abbott are a reminder of the indomitable spirit that God inspires us with. They are an inspiration to me, as I hope they are for you.

Veeck Again

I've already told you about the antics of Bill Veeck, the baseball owner who sent midget Eddie Gaedel to the plate, raised and lowered outfield fences depending on which team was batting, and bought a rocking chair for Satchel Paige so that he could snooze in the bullpen.

But one of Veeck's ideas would have really revolutionized the game. During World War II, when major league rosters were depleted by the war effort, Veeck floated a trial balloon: he would buy the financially strapped Philadelphia Phillies and stock the team with Negro League players. Weren't they the best baseball players left? (A little history lesson here: to add insult to racism, the armed services segregated the races, and many in the Army, Navy, and Air Force considered blacks unfit for combat duty.)

In other words, Veeck would integrate Major League Baseball. *Wait a minute! We can't have that happening! Why, why that wouldn't be right.* That's pretty much the response Veeck received from baseball commissioner Kenesaw Mountain Landis, who stamped out that idea.

They Said It

"Before Eddie Gaedel came along, Bert Shepard was probably the most publicized one-game major leaguer in history when he became the only man ever to pitch in the major leagues with an artificial leg."

—Richard Tellis, author of *Once Around the Bases: Bittersweet Memories of Only One Game in the Majors*

SAY IT AIN'T SO, PETE

44

I sure hope by the time this book comes out that baseball commissioner Bud Selig hasn't decided to reinstate Pete Rose, who has been banned for life from organized baseball.

This sordid and sad story is a cautionary tale about the dangers of gambling. How did it all transpire? To refresh your memory, then-commissioner Bart Giamatti placed Rose's name on baseball's permanently ineligible list in the summer of 1989 following an investigation of Pete's gambling past. Rose hasn't been allowed to appear at an old-timer's game, wear a Major League uniform, work in any capacity for a big league club, or even step on a playing field for the last fifteen years. He can also forget about being inducted into Cooperstown as well; he is ineligible for the Baseball Hall of Fame ballot as long as he's banned from baseball.

There's no doubt that Pete was a great player or deserves a bust alongside the game's greatest players. Besides being the all-time hit king, Rose set eighteen other Major League records, including:

- most games played (3,562)
- most at bats (14,053)
- most singles (3,315)
- being the only player in Major League history to play more than 500 games at five different positions: first base (939), second base (628), third base (634), left field (671), and right field (595)
- producing the longest consecutive-game hitting streak in the National League for the modern era (forty-four games from June 14 through July 31, 1978)

Rose's signature record is the number of hits in a career, and I don't see anyone breaking it. Rose's troubles began three years later when the commissioner's office caught wind of his gambling problems. A six-month investigation ensued. Baseball investigator John Dowd interviewed nine witnesses and received documentation tying Rose to extensive wagering on sports, including baseball. Dowd detailed 412 instances where Rose bet on baseball games, including ones involving the Cincinnati Reds, which he was managing at the time. Betting slips with Rose's signature were produced, as well as a ton of checks to cover his losses.

The losses were significant, even for a multimillionaire like Rose. The Dowd Report alleged that Rose owed as much as $400,000 in one month from baseball bets alone. His gambling habits had come to light when he allegedly welched on some gambling debts, prompting two acquaintances to turn into state's witnesses. Paul Janszen and Ronald Peters, former friends of Rose, met with the baseball investigator and produced the documentation that nailed the game's all-time hit leader. This time around, Charlie Hustle wasn't able to bowl over Bart Giamatti as he did Ray Fosse when he buried his left shoulder into the catcher and scored the winning run in the 1970 All-Star game. (I remember that play. Pete barreled into Fosse—really creamed him—on a bang-bang play at the plate. Fosse hurdled backwards, head over heels, while Rose tagged home with the winning run. It was a clean collision, but Fosse's career was ruined.)

Giamatti had home plate blocked as well. The commissioner banned Rose from baseball for life following the issuance of the Dowd Report in late summer 1989. In an agreement between Giamatti and Rose, the betting ballplayer neither denied or acknowledged that he had bet on any Major League baseball game, but stated that Giamatti acted in good faith throughout the investigation. The report outlined how Rose made $2,000 bets on fifty-two separate Reds games in 1987, and that he bet on baseball in 1985 and 1986, while he was still an active player.

"I know of no evidence to show that Mr. Rose bet against the Reds, [but] in my opinion . . . it doesn't make any difference whether you bet for or against," Giamatti said. "The act of betting on a game you're involved in is, per se, to put yourself at variance with your stated duties. It is to place your desire for monetary gain and therefore perhaps to put your judgment of what should happen on the field ahead of the team's."

Rose crossed a sacred line in my book. He was banned from baseball for violating rule 21(d), which, in part, states: "Any player, umpire, or club or league official or employee, who shall bet any sum upon any baseball game in connection with which the bettor has a duty to perform, shall be permanently ineligible." Rose joins a rogue's gallery of fourteen players who have been banned for life, and he became the first since 1943, when Philadelphia Phillies president William D. Cox was barred for betting on his team. Of course, most baseball fans will never forget the Black Sox scandal of 1919, when Shoeless Joe Jackson and seven other players were banished from the game for "throwing" the 1919 World Series. No player or person who has been banned for life has ever been reinstated, and I urge Commissioner Selig to follow that precedent. Pete Rose shouldn't be in the Hall of Fame, and he shouldn't be part of baseball. Rules are rules, and he knowingly broke a huge one.

I'm afraid I can't generate much sympathy for Charlie Hustle. As of this writing, Rose has shown no repentance for what he has done, has failed to resolve a five-year-old tax lien of $151,000 on his home, and continues to frequent the Strip in Las Vegas, where he was seen gambling in the Bellagio casino and prowling around the sports book at Caesar's Palace.

It's clear to me that Pete has a gambling addiction. Not only has he lost a ton of money (which explains why he still owes the government back taxes), but it's also clear that he's been hooked by gambling. He apparently likes the excitement of laying down big bets on the outcomes of sporting events.

I'm well aware of the dangers of gambling. My good friend and neighbor in Colorado Springs—Dr. James Dobson—served nineteen months on the National Gambling Impact Commission, which raised significant concerns about the negative impacts of gambling in its 1998 report. "This Commission heard testimony that sports wagering is a serious problem that has devastated families and careers," said the report. "Sports wagering threatens the integrity of sports, it puts student athletes in a vulnerable position, it can put adolescent gamblers at risk for gambling problems, and it can devastate individuals and careers."

No lie. We are seeing millions of young people sucked in by gambling all over the country. *Sports Illustrated* ran an article a couple of years ago about the "dirty little secret" on college campuses—rampant betting on football and basketball games that generates much of the energy you see in arenas and stadiums.

Gambling has become so big that Americans visit casinos more often than they attend professional sporting events. Collectively, gamblers lose more than sixty billion dollars a year, which doesn't even begin to describe the human cost. You would probably be surprised at the number of people in your church who've sought counseling regarding their gambling habits. Those who gamble develop a propensity for betting money they can't afford on games they cannot win. We joke about people gambling away the rent money, but it happens more often than you think.

Please, don't allow any sort of gambling to gain a toehold on your life. Even "harmless" scratch-off and state lottery games should be avoided since they are "gateway" games. There are fifteen million compulsive gamblers in this country, who wake up each morning wondering about their next bet—just like Pete Rose. Maybe Pete doesn't want to live that way, but he's hooked by the adrenaline rush that gambling gives him.

The Bible does not speak directly to the subject of gambling, but let me offer two compelling reasons why I think gambling is a bad bet. First, gambling is not biblical because it disrespects honest labor and productive work—major themes espoused in Proverbs. Seeking to get rich in a way that avoids respectable work violates scriptural truth. While you won't find any "Thou shalt nots" in the Bible about laying down a bet on the World Series, Scripture says:

- Gambling encourages greed (Luke 12:15; 1 Timothy 6:10; and Hebrews 13:5).
- Gambling encourages materialism and discontent (Psalm 62:10; 1 Timothy 6:9).
- Gambling discourages honest labor (Proverbs 28:19; 13:11).
- Gambling encourages "get rich quick" thinking (Proverbs 28:20).
- Gambling encourages reckless investment of God-given resources (Matthew 25:14–30).

Second, you're practically guaranteed that you will lose your money. Think of all the tens of millions of dollars that Pete Rose has earned in his lifetime from playing baseball, endorsing products, and signing baseballs at $25 a pop. How many millions has he lost betting on sport events, the roll of the dice, and the turn of a card? Remember, he hasn't erased a $150,000 tax lien on his property yet.

So please, do yourself a favor and stay away from gambling. God will honor your obedience, and you can sleep better at night knowing that you are spending your money on things with a more worthy return—like going to a Major League baseball game with the family.

Now that sounds like a sure bet to me.

It Better Be Made Out of Asbestos

The Cincinnati Reds began playing in one of those fancy new stadiums in 2003—Great American Ball Park. Like many of the new ballparks that have opened their turnstiles in recent years, Great American is a cozier, more intimate, and more attractive place to watch a ball game than Riverfront Stadium ever was. The seats are closer to the field, the sight lines are better, and you have these great cup holders on the seat in front of you.

Pete Rose isn't allowed to step onto the field, but he is allowed to attend games just like any other fan. Even if Pete never sets a foot inside the new stadium, you can't miss his presence at the new ballpark. Pete is featured in an oversized mural of the Reds' 1975 World Series championship team, the year the "Big Red Machine" beat the Boston Red Sox in an exciting seven-game series (Remember Carlton Fisk waving his home-run ball to stay fair?). A pizza parlor at the park is called "Pete's," and one of the private clubs for premium ticket holders was christened Club 4,192. I wonder what they were referring to?

A "quote band" stretches around the circumference of the concourse and includes this memorable line from Pete Rose: "I'd walk through hell in a gasoline suit to keep playing baseball."

I've always appreciated Pete's burning desire to play this great game, so my question to you is: Would you walk through hell in a gasoline suit to keep being a Christian?

Hey, I'm just having a little fun, but that imagery reminds me of Shadrach, Meshach, and Abednego. These three young men defied King Nebuchadnezzar's order to bow and worship the ninety-foot-high gold statue that he had made of himself. This sent King Nebuchadnezzar into a Billy Martin–like rage, and he ordered the three to be pitched into a fiery furnace heated up seven times hotter than usual. God protected the three men inside the superheated furnace. The intense heat had no effect! They rounded the bases and then came home, completely untouched by the flames. Their ball caps weren't singed, and their flannel uniforms were unscorched.

King Nebuchadnezzar knew the home team had won this game, and he ordered everyone in his kingdom to acknowledge God's power and to treat Shadrach, Meshach, and Abednego like All-Stars.

Let's Hope We Never Have to Use This

There's one more thing you should know about the Red's Great American Ball Park: it has a built-in decontamination system to treat fans in case the stadium is subjected to chemical attack.

They Said It

"Pete Rose has gone as far as he's going to go. He won't admit those betting slips were his, but he has vowed to spend the rest of his life searching for the real gamblers."

—Scott Ostler, *San Francisco Chronicle* sports columnist

"It was an embarrassing night. It was like inviting Willie Sutton to a bankers' meeting."

—John Dowd, baseball's investigator in the Pete Rose case, when Rose appeared at the 1999 World Series as a member of the All-Century team

"It was too bad I wasn't a second baseman; then I'd probably have seen a lot more of my husband."

—Karolyn Rose, ex-wife of Pete Rose, in 1981

I've always had a soft spot in my heart for baseball movies—*Field of Dreams, 61*, For the Love of the Game,* and *The Rookie.* There's something about having baseball in the backdrop that just resonates with me. Not that Hollywood always gets it right, but they do a pretty good job, even if you know that the hero will get the final out or stroke the game winning hit in the bottom of the ninth inning.

One baseball movie is especially vivid to me because of my personal connection to it. I'm talking about *The Natural,* which was released twenty years ago. My goodness, has the film really been out that long? It feels like yesterday when I sat down and watched Robert Redford morph into the mythological Roy Hobbs, the home run hitting protagonist with character and principles.

Let me narrate the plot line before I describe my personal involvement with it. It seems that young Roy Hobbs, growing up in the 1920s, can really put the wood on the ball. He eats, drinks, and sleeps baseball in the sleepy Midwest farm town in which he grows up. He learns the game from the knee of his father, a salt-of-the-earth farmer with rock-ribbed values. In a telling scene early in the movie, lightning strikes a tree, splitting it open. Young Roy carves his own bat from the splintered wood, which is obviously imbued with something special. He names the bat "Wonder Boy." I think director Barry Levinson was playing off imagery of how Moses received the Ten Commandments—a burst of lightning, and then the hand of God writes on stone tablets for the ages.

It turns out that Roy is more than a slugger; he has quite an arm, too. A barnstorming troupe of major leaguers pass through, and the bet is made that Roy can strike out a Babe Ruth–lookalike slugger known as "The Whammer." Naturally, Roy blows him away, which earns him a tryout with the Chicago Cubs.

Once in the big city, the naïve farm boy falls prey to a world full of temptations, including the temptress Harriet Bird (Barbara Hershey), a deranged woman whose mission in life is to snuff out the most promising prospects. This honey pot lures Hobbs to her bed, where she shoots the youth in the chest with a silver bullet, leaving him for dead. She acts like Delilah when she found Samson's weakness, and Harriet defrocks the young player just as Delilah cut Samson's famous locks to take away his strength.

Hobbs disappears from baseball, only to emerge sixteen years later as a thirtysomething rookie with the worst team in the major leagues—the 1939 New York Knights. A crusty old coot named Pop (Wilford Brimley) manages this collection of misfits, but he is loath to play the long-in-the-tooth rookie. "You don't start playing ball at your age," he tells Hobbs. "You retire."

Whenever Hobbs gets a chance to pinch hit, he sends rockets into the alleys and clubs majestic home runs into the second deck of—wait a minute, I recognize that stadium. That's War Memorial Stadium in Buffalo, New York! I *pitched* in that classically styled stadium for two seasons with the Buffalo Bisons, the Pittsburgh Pirates Double A team. War Memorial, with its tall, brooding grandstands, was a throwback to the bandbox ball fields of yesterday. I'm talking about places like the Polo Grounds and Ebbets Field, where fans perched in the second deck seemed to sit on top of you. I loved War Memorial's old-time atmosphere—but I hated the infield dirt and short right field fence.

I think the last time War Memorial's infield was raked was when Bobby Thompson hit the "Shot Heard Round the World" in the 1951 playoffs between the New York Giants and the Brooklyn Dodgers. Ground balls ricocheted off rocks the size of peach pits, and our infielders nicknamed it the "Rockyard."

What I remember most about War Memorial was the right field porch just 285 feet down the line. That was a pitcher's nightmare. I chuckled during the movie when I noticed that they had painted a "310" on the wall. *Yeah, right. If they only knew how many pop flies I saw duck into the right field bleachers.*

Roy Hobbs, a left-handed hitter, doesn't need a short porch. He smashes home run after home run with a combination of power and grace as the inspirational score by Randy Newman swells in the background. He gets his chance to play every day when the Knights' right fielder crashes into the outfield fence and dies. (I told you this was a Hollywood movie.) With Hobbs pounding the ball, the improbable Knights make a run for the pennant. The movie is filled with all sorts of shadowy characters, from the black-clad Harriet Bird to a crooked team owner. But I was fascinated with the way director Barry Levinson treats Iris (played by Glenn Close), Hobbs's old girlfriend. When the slugger is in the midst of a slump, Iris—bathed in heavenly streaks of light—stands up in Wrigley Field in a white dress and a hat on her head that looks like a halo. Hobbs swivels his head and holds her in awe.

The climactic, bottom-of-the-ninth scene departs from reality. I forget the exact details, but with two men on and two out, Roy needs a booming blast for the Knights to win the pennant. As with sports movies, the action slows down . . . as . . . left-handed hitter Roy digs in and studies the pitcher through a furrowed brow. In his hands is "Wonder Boy," the special homemade bat that had been at his side since his sandlot days. (major league bats rarely last more than a week or two before breaking, but this is Hollywood, remember?) With a one-one count, Roy swings from his heels . . . and it could be . . . it could be . . . "Foul!" yells the home plate ump as the ball disappears into the second deck of the right field bleachers.

Roy returns to the plate where he receives the shock of his life: "Wonder Boy" lies shattered in pieces. His prized bat, the one he has treated like Excalibur, is ready for the toothpick factory.

This is the part of the movie that I love. Roy picks up the broken pieces and hands them to the fresh-faced batboy. He jerks his head toward the bat rack. "Go pick me out a winner, Bobby," he says.

With a new bat in his hands—a bat he has never swung in anger before—Roy turns on the next pitch. In super-slow motion, we watch the bat strike the ball, which is sent into a small orbit high above the second deck. The music swells, the ball strikes the bank of lights, and a rainstorm of electrical sparks showers the field as Roy rounds the bases.

And Roy hits his home run without "Wonder Boy"! What a great metaphor for how we can live the Christian life. It may not happen to all of us, but some day something you trust in—real estate, a career, even your health—will shatter into a thousand pieces, just like Roy's prized bat. Who or what will you trust in then?

My left arm was taken from me, and believe me, I trusted in that arm. My left arm had been my strength—my ticket into the big leagues. That arm had delivered pitches that confounded some of the game's best hitters. That arm signed contracts that paid me well to play a game that I loved. That arm wrapped around the loves of my life—Jan and our two children. Then I lost that arm, and now there's nothing there but empty space.

I've admitted how I battled depression after the amputation. I've disclosed how crummy it was to lose an arm the way I did. But at the end of the day, I had to place my trust in Christ. It was the only way I could get up in the morning. This verse from Proverbs says it all: "Listen to this wise advice; follow it closely, for it will do you good, and you can pass it on to others: *Trust in the Lord*" (22:17–19, TLB).

Now that's a great pitch.

Baseball's Version of Murphy's Law

I bet you've never heard of "Koppett's Law," which states: "Whatever creates the greatest inconvenience for the largest number must happen."

Leonard Koppett, a baseball writer of note until his death in 2003, wrote the law. Born in Moscow, Russia, in 1923, Koppett came to the United States at the age of five and grew up one block from Yankee Stadium. His sportswriting career began with the *New York Herald-Tribune* in 1948, and in 1963, the Gray Lady in Pinstripes—the *New York Times*—picked him up on waivers. He wrote a ton of newspaper and magazine articles about baseball over the years, plus the book, *Thinking Man's Guide to Baseball*.

Here's what Koppett's Law means in baseball terms. If the Atlanta Braves and the San Francisco Giants are playing Game 4 of the National League Championship Series in Atlanta, the team that's behind 2–1 in the best-of-five series will win because both teams will have to fly cross-country *that night* to play Game 5 in San Francisco the next day. That's Koppett's Law, inconveniencing the most people possible.

So remember that the next time life hassles you. I like to think that God allows inconveniences to happen in our lives so that we can be drawn near to him and experience his strength to help us endure "stuff" that happens in our lives. "Draw near to God, and He will draw near to you," says James 4:8 (NASB), which is great advice to recall when Koppett's Law strikes.

They Said It

"I watch a lot of baseball on the radio."

—Gerald Ford, president of the United States

THE DAY THE EARTH SHOOK
IN A WORLD SERIOUS WAY

46

You know how people say they can remember where they were when Kennedy was shot or when terrorists flew passenger airlines into the World Trade Center on September 11, 2001?

Those were horrible, tragic events. I'll never forget being in my Colorado Springs home on September 11 and watching—live—the second airplane strike the World Trade Center. The memory of the nuns announcing in my third-grade classroom that President Kennedy had been shot in Dallas is something I will also never forget, just as I will never forget the World Series earthquake on October 17, 1989, in San Francisco.

Remember that tragedy? A powerful earthquake rocked the San Francisco Bay Area less than a half hour before the start of Game 3 of the 1989 World Series. We were playing our cross-bay rivals, the Oakland Athletics.

Here's what happened that day. I had spent the morning at the doctor's office in nearby Palo Alto reviewing X rays of a *second* fracture in my left arm. The first fracture had come during my second comeback game two months earlier in Montreal—that famous pitch where I fell to the ground like a rag doll after my left arm audibly and sickeningly snapped in two. Then I broke my arm *again* when we won the National League playoffs against the poor Chicago Cubs, just like in 1984 when I was with San Diego. I was dressed in a Giant uniform, my arm wrapped in a sleeve, and I was sitting in the Giants dugout when Ryne Sandberg bounced a ground ball to second base to end the game.

If you've seen it once, you've seen it a million times: our team sprinted out of the dugout as if someone had lit a dynamite fuse and tossed it our way. I was leading the charge, even though I had a broken arm on the mend and should have known better. In the pandemonium, I ended up in a big dog pile of players when suddenly, I was jolted from behind. The next thing I knew, I experienced the most searing pain in my left arm. I crouched down and tried to protect myself in the mayhem until a couple of players noticed how much pain I was in. They lifted me out the scrum and led me off the field. I cradled my left arm as my teammates continued to hug and wrestle each other to the ground.

The second arm break hurt more than the Montreal snap-to. My doctor informed me that morning before Game 3 of the World Series that my arm had not suffered any permanent damage. Long-term, I would be okay, he said, but I had definitely set back my recovery.

I returned to my apartment to find Jan dealing with a telephone that rang every time she set it back down. If close friends and long-lost acquaintances weren't calling us for tickets, it was another reporter asking me for an update on the arm. Jan and I were mentally fried by the time we set out for Candlestick Park.

First pitch was set for 5:25 p.m. local time. For mid-October, the fall evening was turning out to be rather balmy. A light sweater was all fans needed, which was quite a contrast to how cool and gloomy Candlestick can usually get, even in the summer. As locals were fond of saying, the coldest winter Mark Twain ever spent was a summer in San Francisco.

Jan, my parents, and some friends took their field level seats behind the Giants dugout while I walked to the dressing room. I was still suiting up for each game—the best seat in the house is the dugout, right?—although I was careful to make sure that nobody bumped into me.

I sat down next to my locker and kibitzed with Bob Knepper, one of the "God Squad" members. I can't remember what we were talking about, but then we heard a low rumble. We looked at each other. At first blush, I thought a large passenger jet had made a low pass over the stadium. In a second or two, it became apparent that the rumbling noise was something far different than a jet in the wrong airspace.

"That's an earthquake, Dave," said Bob.

"It *is* an earthquake," I agreed.

What can you do? Growing up in Ohio, we were used to tornadoes and twisters and the heads-up notice the Weather Bureau gave you. But in California, earthquakes come out of nowhere, and there's nothing you can do about it, except stand in a doorway perhaps.

That's what some players started doing as the rumbling turned into a violent shaking of the locker room. The thought flashed through my mind that we were in the bowels of Candlestick Park with massive amounts of concrete and steel girder above us. At that instant, Bob and I sprinted for the exit and into the player's parking lot.

The players were besieged by reporters for a reaction. Some of the TV guys said they had heard that the Bay Bridge went down, which certainly made me sit up and pay attention. Another said downtown San Francisco was on fire and this was the Quake of '06 all over again. Then the lights went out. That's when I knew I had to find Jan.

Since the lights were out in the tunnel leading from the locker room to the field, I felt along the wall with my right hand until I stumbled out onto the field, which was lit by a setting sun.

Everywhere I looked on the diamond, I saw players and coaches in knots, talking about what had just happened. A weird buzz came from the stands, which were half full, I would say. The scoreboard was blank from the lack of electricity.

I looked for Jan and found her in my section, but she was too far back from the field to hear me. She put her right hand to her right ear and pretended to talk. *Telephone*. Right, I nodded. I understood her mime: we needed to telephone the babysitter back at the apartment to be sure the kids were all right.

This was before cell phones were as common as money clips. I worked my way through the pitch-black tunnel back to the clubhouse, but it was dark in there. Then I remembered that Atlee Hammaker, another "God Squad" teammate, had one of those newfangled car phones. I hoofed it out to the players' parking lot and found Atlee among the teeming chaos, but he told me the phone lines were tied up.

I returned to the field, where security personnel had allowed players' families to gather. I hugged Jan, who was clearly scared. "David, I'm really worried about Tiffany and Jonathan," she said, trying to keep panic from rising in her throat.

I nodded my head. We had no idea how bad the damage had been outside the 'Stick.

"I'll meet you in the parking lot," I said, and I hustled back to the locker room to change into regular clothes. Several clubhouse attendants had flashlights going to help us get dressed.

The exit from the Candlestick parking lot seemed slower than usual. As we inched forward, we saw nothing but black hills above the Bayshore Freeway. That was eerie.

We drove to Foster City, where our neighborhood was one of the few with lights on. Our children, seven and four at the time, were just fine. They had been swimming in the complex pool when the earthquake struck. The water sloshed around the pool like if Shamu had done a belly flop, but when the water kept sloshing back and forth, they panicked a bit. A neighbor dived into the pool and helped them to safety.

We were safe and sound, but when we watched the TV coverage, we realized that some poor folks would never come home. Others would have miraculous stories to tell of how God spared their lives.

One of those stories involves a Giants baseball fan named Mike Redlick, who worked at Safeway supermarket's corporate headquarters in Oakland as a logistics analyst. Mike lived in South San Francisco, so he enjoyed a "reverse commute" when he drove home from work every evening: he drove *into* San Francisco at the end of every workday before driving south out of the city to his San Bruno home.

Mike left work a few minutes before 5:00 p.m., glad that he would be driving on Cypress Freeway—Interstate 880—toward the San Francisco Bay Bridge instead of slugging it out on the Bayshore Freeway, the main artery that had to be clogged with commuters and fans trying to get to Candlestick.

Mike tuned his radio to the pregame show as he veered his '84 Pontiac Sunbird into the flowing traffic, which seemed to be a tad lighter than usual. Usually the four lanes were jammed with cars until the Bay Bridge was in sight. On this afternoon, the traffic was moving along rather well, so he figured that he would make good time. By the time he reached the Bayshore Freeway and passed Candlestick, all the fans would be seated for the first pitch, and from there it would be clear sailing. His pregnant wife, Lynn, would be waiting for him at home, along with his two preschool-age boys, Matt and Sean.

Mike was a road warrior: his root-beer colored four-door Pontiac had plenty of commuting miles on the odometer. The Cypress Freeway was a double-decked structure. The top deck was a four-lane expressway running south toward San Jose. The middle deck was reserved for northbound traffic. Beneath the freeway, surface streets crossed in east-west grids.

Mike stepped on the gas and easily merged into lane two of the northbound middle deck. Suddenly Mike felt someone bump his car from behind. Had he been rear-ended? Then all four tires felt as if someone had let the air out of them. As his mind was struggling to process what this meant, he was flung *sideways,* crashing into the passenger-side window and breaking it. He had been wearing his seat belt, so his body was half-in the car and half-out the passenger window. A very awkward position to be in, to be sure.

Dazed, Mike focused his eyes and struggled to figure out what had just happened. He definitely wasn't going anywhere. He soon determined why: slabs of concrete entombed his car, with one huge chunk nested atop the front hood of the Pontiac. The weird thing was that his engine was still running. In his dazed confusion, Mike thought he heard a frantic voice on the radio announcing that a major earthquake had struck the Bay Area.

Mike struggled to snap his mind into gear. Blood dropped down his forehead and onto his face, but as he moved around a bit, he didn't feel any broken bones. It began to come together: he was pinned precariously under tons of concrete, and there was nothing that Mike could do to rescue himself.

"God, you're in control here," he prayed. "If you want to take me, it's in your hands. You know that I have a beautiful wife, two kids, another on the way, but if it's your will that I not survive, I give myself to you."

Acrid dust swirled through the air, causing difficulty to breathe. Mike yelled out for help, but part of him thought that any sort of rescue was hopeless.

The top deck of the Cypress Freeway had "pancaked" and fallen onto the lower deck, crushing cars and their occupants. Residents from nearby neighborhoods ran to the wrecked freeway because they could see pockets where the top deck had not completely flattened the northbound deck. Many of these Good Samaritans began climbing shattered support columns in an effort to reach the trapped victims, who could be heard yelling for help.

In what had to seem like an eternity for Mike, he continued to scream for assistance while praying that God would spare his life. He wondered whether a sharp aftershock would bring the entire freeway structure down to ground level.

Then he heard a couple of guys working their way toward him. "Oh, Jesus, have mercy!" one of his rescuers said to a buddy. "Somebody is alive!"

Three men reached Mike, who told them that he couldn't budge the door open.

"I'll be right back," said one of the rescuers, who returned a few minutes later with a crow bar.

They took turns working the door until they finally sprung it open and freed Mike. They assisted Mike out of the vehicle and helped him climb out of the collapsed freeway, where he sat down on a nearby sidewalk, understandably in shock. He felt soreness in his chest, several teeth had been chipped, but he was going to be okay. Everywhere he looked he saw scenes that reminded him of a Hollywood disaster film. A five-mile-long stretch of the Cypress Freeway had been reduced to rubble, crushing forty-one people and injuring scores of others, including some who had to have their legs sawed off in order to be freed.

Paramedics whisked Mike to a nearby hospital, where he was treated and released. At 8:00 p.m., he phoned Lynn, who had not realized that he had been trapped under the Cypress Freeway. A cousin from the East Bay offered to drive him home.

As their car sped across the undamaged San Mateo Bridge, Mike reflected on the moment. He could have—he should have—been dead in an earthquake that measured 6.9 on the Richter scale. Instead, God had spared his life. Why did that happen? Why was he so fortunate to live when others died?

The more he thought about it, the more he realized that God orchestrated some unusual circumstances to keep him alive. Why was he thrown sideways when the car came to a sudden halt? All the crash-dummy slow-motion replays of wrecks show mannequins being launched *forward*. Why had he gone sideways when he was wearing a seat belt? And why wasn't the Pontiac totally crushed by tons of concrete that landed on his hood and roof?

The only answer that Mike could come up with was that he had been given a new lease on life, and it was up to him how he would use that special gift as a husband and a father.

Those were similar feelings that hit me like a ton of bricks—not tons of concrete like it did for Mike—when I heard my doctor inform me that I had cancer. Suddenly, I found myself playing on a very foreign field.

The field I was about to play on had no lines to define where the game would be played against cancer. I didn't know how many outs there were to an inning. I didn't know how long I'd get to play against cancer. I didn't know if I was going to win or lose.

That type of thinking was so foreign to me. As a pitcher, I was used to being in control. The game of baseball cannot be played until the pitcher throws the ball. On the playing field against cancer, however, I had no control. Cancer was throwing the pitches, and they were pitches I was not familiar with. As a batter, I was used to seeing fastballs, curveballs, and change-ups, but with cancer, I had no clue what was coming my way.

That was scary. I had to learn that God was in control and leave the outcome to him.

For an old baseball player, that was hard to do, but I'm a much better person for having played against cancer.

They Said It

"We want to be very sensitive, as you would expect us to be, as to the state of life in this community. The great tragedy is that it coincides with our modest little sporting event."

—Baseball commissioner Fay Vincent, speaking to reporters hours after the earthquake struck the San Francisco area on October 17, 1989

BRANCH RICKEY'S
SECRET AMBITION

47

If William Wilberforce was a giant of the Christian faith, then his baseball counterpart would have to be Branch Rickey.

William Wilberforce, an English statesman and a Christian who lived from 1759–1833, campaigned for the abolition of the slave trade throughout the British Empire. He is generally credited with inspiring the abolitionist movement in this country, which eventually led to the Civil War and the Emancipation Proclamation of 1863, effectively setting all slaves free.

In a similar fashion, Branch Rickey, owner and general manager of the Brooklyn Dodgers in the 1940s, single-handedly emancipated an entire race to play Major League baseball and ended one of the game's most notorious and unfair edicts: that black players need not apply when it came to playing the great game of baseball. It was Mr. Rickey who signed modern baseball's first black player, Jackie Robinson, and navigated the rocky shoals of integrating the National Pastime.

The reason I compare Branch Rickey with William Wilberforce is because Mr. Rickey's evangelical faith influenced his actions and propelled him to desegregate baseball. Born the son of a Methodist preacher in 1881, Mr. Rickey grew up in a Christian home and promised his mother that he would never play baseball on Sundays. (Back in those days, very few teams played baseball on the Sabbath.)

Mr. Rickey attended a Methodist college—Ohio Wesleyan University—and coached the baseball team when he was twenty-two years old. Nearly one hundred years ago (in April 1904), the team traveled to South Bend, Indiana, to play Notre Dame. Even in those days, Ohio Wesleyan fielded an integrated team—their catcher and lone black player was Charles Thomas.

Mr. Rickey's team pulled into South Bend following a long train ride and immediately checked into a local hotel. The hotel clerk took one look at Charles and said, "I have rooms for all of you—except for him," jerking his head toward the black player.

"Why don't you have a room for him?" Mr. Rickey asked.

"Because the hotel policy is whites only."

"Can Charlie stay in my room?" Branch asked. "Surely you can find a cot for me."

It took all of Mr. Rickey's verbal skills to talk the hotel clerk into letting Charles Thomas stay with him. After everyone got squared away, Mr. Rickey called a team meeting.

As everyone sat in a semicircle, Charlie bowed his head and cried as though his heart would break. Then he started pulling frantically at the skin on his hands and forearms, saying, "Black skin . . . black skin . . . if only I could make it white." Mr. Rickey later told his grandson that he had witnessed the saddest sight that day: a black man crying his eyes out while he tried vainly to rub the black skin off his forearms by sheer friction.

That scene resonated in Mr. Rickey's memory. After his coaching stint at Ohio Wesleyan, Mr. Rickey resumed his playing days. He was a good enough catcher to play parts of four seasons with the St. Louis Browns and the New York Highlanders (later the Yankees), getting into 120 games and batting .239 lifetime before a shoulder injury cut short his career.

He loved baseball and was determined to find himself a place in the front office. Mr. Rickey turned out to be a genius and an innovator decades ahead of his time. When he became the general manager of the St. Louis Cardinals in the 1930s, he invented the farm system. Believe it or not, finding baseball talent was a hit-or-miss concept in those days; would-be hopefuls latched on to semipro teams or caught the eye of scouts beating the bushes in the countryside. The idea of a cohesive minor league farm system developing talent that could be harvested by the parent club was unheard of until Mr. Rickey came along. He "farmed out" players to a network of thirty-two minor league clubs, in effect, controlling a "chain gang" of some six hundred players.

As shrewd a baseball mind as they came, "The Mahatma," as Tom Meany of the *New York World Telegram* called him, was a teetotaler who liked to wear black suits and bow ties. Mr. Rickey kept a hawk-like eye on ballplayers from the casual ball toss hours before the game until the final out. Many baseball observers said that he became the best judge of baseball talent in the first half of the twentieth century. He was an innovator in other ways as well: Mr. Rickey came up with the idea of pitching machines, sliding pits, batting helmet, batting cages, and erecting rectangular lines of string over the plate so that a pitcher could throw to a strike-zone target. When he later joined the Dodgers, he turned an old naval base in Vero Beach, Florida, into Dodgertown, a four-diamond complex where players could get some real work done during spring training.

But the Mahatma could never forget the sight of a dejected black man lamenting something he had no control over—the color of his skin. The scout in him told him that the Negro Leagues of the 1930s harbored some great athletic talent. But as long as Judge Kenesaw Mountain Landis was commissioner of baseball, blacks would be barred from the game. He consistently blocked any attempts to allow black players inside the lines. The last time organized baseball had a black player was in 1901, when John J. McGraw, manager of the Baltimore Orioles (then a minor league team), tried to pass off Charlie Grant, a second baseman in the Negro Leagues graced with high cheekbones and straight hair, as a Native American named Charles Tokohama. Sorry, Charlie.

In the early 1940s, some baseball people like Brooklyn manager Leo Durocher said they would love to have "colored players" on their team (so they could win), but baseball's "unwritten rule" tied their hands. When asked about this, Judge Landis said in lawyerly language, "There is no rule, formal or informal, in any understanding—unwritten, subterranean, or sub-anything—against the hiring of Negro players by the teams of organized baseball. Negroes are not barred from organized baseball—never have been in the twenty-one years I have served."

Not barred? How does this explain what happened to Bill Veeck when he showed that he was serious about buying the cash-strapped Philadelphia Phillies in 1943 and stocking the roster with players from the Negro League? Not only did Commissioner Landis and the other baseball owners quickly extinguish that rebel idea, they orchestrated a situation in which two days after Veeck made his purchase offer, National League president Ford Frick sold the Phillies for less than *half* of Veeck's offering price to someone willing to maintain the status quo. That's how desperate the owners were to keep black players off major league rosters.

A few months after the Phillies debacle, Branch Rickey purchased the Brooklyn Dodgers and took on the role of owner/general manager. He confided to his wife, Jane, that he was thinking of integrating baseball. She pleaded with him not to try, not because she opposed integration, but she felt the challenge would be too great. Someone younger, she argued, should carry that heavy burden. Besides, she said, his critics had called him "El Cheapo" for years because of the way he wheeled and dealed his players to other clubs, crying poverty. "This will be one more slander on your name," she said.

Mr. Rickey could never erase the sight of Charles Thomas, bawling like a baby and cursing the color of skin. "I couldn't face God much longer, knowing that his black creatures are held separate and distinct from his white creatures in the game that has given me all I own," he told his grandson years later.

So Mr. Rickey started his secret ambition. He let it be known that the Dodgers were thinking of forming a Negro League team to play in Ebbets Field when the Dodgers were out on the road. The black team would be known as the Brown Dodgers, said the Mahatma, who directed his scouts to look over one hundred players in the Negro Leagues. He needed to stock his new team, right?

Nobody knew that his scouts were looking for that special person to break the color barrier. He had to be a great player—not someone who would ride the pine on a major league bench—but a star, an impact player whose talent was beyond dispute. There were political and sociological considerations that also had to be factored in: baseball's first black player couldn't be seen as "uppity"—a phrase used at the time to describe (in white people's eyes) black people who didn't know their place. His character, like Caesar's wife, had to be above reproach. He had to be married or least have a serious black girlfriend. And finally, the black ballplayer had to be dark-skinned, as in *really* black. When Major League Baseball was integrated, Mr. Rickey wanted everyone to know that a black ballplayer was taking the field.

The Brooklyn scouts bird-dogged the Negro Leagues and determined there were at least eight black players who were big league locks: outfielders Cool Papa Bell and Sam Jethroe, shortstop Piper Davis, second basemen Marvin Williams and Jackie Robinson, first baseman Buck Leonard, and catchers Josh Gibson and Roy Campanella. As I've described earlier in this book, Satchel Paige, the ageless string-bean pitcher who had dazzled batters for two decades, was deemed past his prime.

And then the mountain moved. Judge Kenesaw Mountain Landis, the baseball commissioner who stood in the way of integration (and was certainly told to take that stance by the other fifteen club owners), died in 1944. A. B. "Happy" Chandler, a former governor and U.S. Senator from Kentucky, replaced him.

Branch Rickey thought the timing was right, and he had Happy Chandler's support as well. As America's troops were coming home from the long, exhaustive war against the Axis Powers, the new baseball commissioner said that if black people "can fight and die on

Okinawa, Guadalcanal, and in the South Pacific, they can play ball in America."

Mr. Rickey found his man for what he called "The Noble Experiment." He was Jackie Robinson, whose skin was as black as coal and whose baseball talent and personal integrity could not be denied. On August 28, 1945, Mr. Rickey signed Jackie Robinson to a contract to play baseball, but the signing was kept under wraps until after the World Series on October 23, 1945. The signing of Jackie Robinson rocked the baseball world, but the Brooklyn owner had some political cover: the New York State Legislature had recently passed the Quinn-Ives Act prohibiting discrimination in hiring, and New York City colorful mayor Fiorello LaGuardia was sitting on an "End Jim Crow in Baseball" committee.

The press immediately wanted to know what Mr. Rickey's plans were for organized baseball's first black player since 1901. They were told that Robinson would train with the Dodgers during spring training in Vero Beach, Florida, and play the 1946 season for the Dodgers' Triple A team in Montreal.

I'll have more to say about Jackie Robinson in my next chapter, but don't think for one minute that baseball was integrated one-two-three following Jackie's signing. Racist thinking dies hard. Montreal Royals manager Clay Hopper had a question for Mr. Rickey: "Do you really think that a nigger is a human being?"

Well, sure, Clay, of course he is. . . .

During spring training in 1946, the Dodgers took Jackie along to Jacksonville, Florida, to play an exhibition game. When the team bus arrived, they were told that the game was canceled because the lights weren't working. The first pitch was scheduled for noon that day.

Jackie silenced the critics that a "nigger" couldn't play baseball on opening day with the Dodger's farm team in Montreal. He went four-for-five with a home run, two stolen bases, and four runs scored in a 14–1 rout for the Royals. Oh, and the pitcher in me has to note that he caused two balks.

During the 1946 season in Montreal, he batted .349, with 133 runs and 40 stolen bases, but more importantly, he helped the Royals draw a club-record 412,744 fans at home and nearly 400,000 on the road.

The stage was set to bring up Jackie for the 1947 season, and here's where Branch Rickey needed all of his godly wisdom. Remember: Major League Baseball still had this "unwritten" rule—no blacks. He petitioned the baseball owners to be "allowed" to play Jackie, and their response was to hold a secret meeting to hear out Mr. Rickey and then put the matter up to a vote. After hearing his case, several of the owners said that they wanted to take an "orderly course" in handling the Negro question. Three owners had been appointed to sit on a "policy committee," and they would get to the issue in due time.

When Mr. Rickey pressed for a vote, he got one: 15–1 against him. Everyone in the room understood, however, that if the news slipped out that they had taken a vote on Jackie Robinson, there would be a lot of explaining to do, especially in northern cities, where integration was further along than in the South. So ballots and notes from that meeting were destroyed.

Meanwhile, outside the smoked-filled back room where the commissioners met, there were rumors that the St. Louis Cardinals and the Philadelphia Phillies would refuse to play if Jackie Robinson was in the lineup. Branch Rickey knew he had National League president Ford Frick in his corner. "I don't care if half the league strikes," said the NL president. "All will be suspended, and I do not care if it wrecks the National League for five years. This is the United States of America, and one citizen has as much right to play as another."

The person needed to break the stalemate was the new baseball commissioner. Now, you wouldn't think that a former U.S. Senator from a Southern state—a person who went around saying "Ah love baseball"—would prove to be sympathetic to bringing down the wall barring blacks from Major League Baseball. But Chandler ordered the owners to let it happen—Jackie could play.

Jackie broke the color barrier on April 18, 1947, with a home game at Ebbets Field. That went well, but it was the team's first road trip that had everyone holding their breath. The Philadelphia Phillies were making noises that Jackie wouldn't be welcome in the City of Brotherly Love, a city where Jackie had no problem playing before thousands of black fans when he was shortstop of the Kansas City Monarchs.

Harold Parrott, the traveling secretary for the Dodgers and the person responsible for booking hotel rooms and coordinating the travel, was called into Branch Rickey's office. He recounts this story in his insightful book, *The Lords of Baseball*. The Mahatma, who was on the phone, urged his traveling secretary to pick up a second phone so that he could listen in to the conversation.

On the line was Herb Pennock, the Phillies General Manager who was a great southpaw for the Yankees.

". . . just can't bring the nigger here with the rest of the team, Branch," Parrott overheard Pennock saying. "We're just not ready for that sort of thing yet. We won't be able to take the field against your Brooklyn team if that boy Robinson is in uniform."

"Very well, Herbert," replied the always-precise Dodger owner. "And if we must claim the game nine to nothing, we will do just that, I assure you."

Forfeited games go down in the books as a 9–0 victory.

When the Dodger team got off the train in Philadelphia, they took cabs to the Benjamin Franklin Hotel, a hotel that Parrott described as "second-rate" and a place where the Dodgers had stayed for years. A month earlier, Parrott had mailed down a rooming list, which included Robinson's name, and hadn't heard a peep of protest.

With the Dodger team milling around the lobby, Parrott was told that there was no room at the inn. "And don't bring your team back here," the hotel manager snapped, "while you have any nigras with you!"

With their luggage stacked on the sidewalk, the traveling secretary wondered what to do. He called the Phillies front office for some help, but no one would take his call, so Parrott sent the players to the ballpark and said he'd work on finding them a place to stay. One of the Dodger players asked Robinson if he had some friends in town who'd take in the team as boarders. Jackie managed a weak smile, but it was obvious to all that the incident was tearing him up.

The Dodger traveling secretary went on a hotel hunt. He almost didn't stop at the second hotel, the Warwick, because it looked too plush. When Parrott explained his little "problem," the hotel manager said they were delighted to have them stay. Of course, the rate was twice as much as the Benjamin Franklin, but it was safe harbor during a stormy time.

The Dodgers, led by Branch Rickey, stayed the course. Jackie had a very good year in 1947, batting .297, hitting 12 home runs, batting in 125 runs, stealing 29 bases, and being named Rookie of the Year. His success paved the way for more teams to integrate, although it took the Boston Red Sox *ten years* to become the last team to add a black player to the roster.

Branch Rickey opened the door for thousands of black players—*and* Hispanic and Latino players—to play Major League Baseball. What many people don't know is that Mr. Rickey also played a part in paving the way for perhaps hundreds of thousands, if not millions, of young people to come to know Christ. In 1954, Mr. Rickey cofounded the Fellowship of Christian Athletes, which has been challenging coaches and athletes on the professional, college, high school, junior high, and youth levels to use athletics to impact the world for Jesus Christ. The FCA is the largest Christian sports organization in America, equipping, empowering, and encouraging people to make a difference for Christ.

Branch Rickey, especially in his latter years, couldn't stop talking about Jesus Christ. He often returned to the Ohio Wesleyan campus to speak to students and then be available to talk afterward. That's when he would take out his cigar, often leaving it unlit, and using the cigar as a prop as he proceeded to tell baseball stories that eventually became a launching pad to stories about Jesus and the importance of doing things his way, no matter what the cost.

I never got to meet Branch Rickey; he died in 1965 at the age of eighty-three while giving a speech at the Sports Hall of Fame in Columbus, Ohio. At that event, Mr. Rickey was working hard to tell the story of Jesus calling Zacchaeus. Known as bit of a rambler speaker who took a while to get to his point, Mr. Rickey said, "I don't believe I can finish the story."

Those were his last words.

But Mr. Rickey, you didn't need to finish the story. You were a faithful servant who did the game of baseball a tremendous service at a time when nobody was willing to join your crusade.

His Name Lives On

I have met Mr. Rickey's grandson and namesake, Branch Rickey, who lives in my hometown of Colorado Springs, Colorado, where he is president of the Pacific Coast League. One time I ran into him at a Sky Sox game (that's the Triple A affiliate for the Colorado Rockies), and it was fun to sit next to him and talk baseball.

Branch is a wonderful man who is cut from the same cloth as his famous grandfather. He was the assistant farm director for the Pittsburgh Pirates when I signed out of college, and I think he was in the office when I inked that contract and became a professional ballplayer. While Branch was with the Pittsburgh organization, he established a new policy: whenever one of the farm teams decided to release or send down a player, that had to be a unanimous decision by the coaching staff. Branch knew that when you released a kid, it was like saying, "The dream is over, buddy." That's why when he delivered the tough news, he wanted to be able to tell the player that he had talked to each coach, that it had been a unanimous decision, and that he regretted that the player was not a good fit in the organization.

I think players can deal with their disappointment much better when it's handled this way. I can still remember the keen sense of disappointment I felt when I retired, hung up my spikes, called it a career, walked away from the game, said adios to baseball, or whatever cliché you want to insert. The date was November 13, 1989, three months from the time I broke my arm pitching in Montreal and just one month after I broke it a second time during the wild on-the-field celebration when we won the National League pennant against the Chicago Cubs. I had just learned from my doctor that a large lump had appeared above the location of the previous tumor.

The dream that I was living—pitching in the major leagues—was over. I had to leave a game and a style of life that gave me such great pleasure to be a part of.

It still hurts to think about that day, as it does for all ballplayers who pack up their belongings for the last time. I'm happy that Branch has taken a proactive step to soften the blow.

What an Honor

Did you know that the Major League Baseball Players Alumni Association and the Rotary Club of Denver have been handing out the "Branch Rickey Award" since 1991? The award is given annually to an outstanding individual in Major League Baseball who could be an owner, manager, or part of the front office personnel. He is supposed to be a role model for others as evidenced by his baseball accomplishments, coupled with high ethical standards.

Past winners have been all players, however. Ozzie Smith, Tony Gwynn, Brett Butler, Paul Molitor, and Curt Schilling are just a few of the past honorees.

They Said It

"Luck is the residue of design."

—Branch Rickey

He that will not reason is a bigot.

He that cannot reason is a fool.

He that dares not reason is a slave.

—A saying hung in Branch Rickey's office

"If Branch Rickey were alive today,
he'd be spinning in his grave."

—New York Mets broadcaster Ralph Kiner on the state
of the Dodgers and baseball in 1999

THE JACKIE ROBINSON STORY 48

"I don't know nothing about no Jackie Robinson," said Vince Coleman, a black ballplayer for the St. Louis Cardinals in a 1986 interview.

Joe Black, a former Brooklyn Dodgers teammate of Jackie and black himself, was, shall we say, more than mildly disturbed that a modern player of color wasn't aware of Jackie's pioneering efforts.

So Black wrote Coleman a letter, which said: "Are black athletes so blinded by greed for dollars and ego trips that they fail to remember that someone had to open the doors? Vince, Jackie Robinson was more than an athlete. He was a man. Jackie Robinson stood alone as he challenged and integrated modern-day Major League Baseball. His task was not easy nor quick. He suffered many mental and physical hurts, he accepted and overcame the slings, slams, and insults so that young black youths, such as you, could dream of playing Major League Baseball."

Jackie Robinson suffered greatly for what he did. I'll never forget watching a made-for-TV movie back in 1997—the fiftieth anniversary of Jackie's rookie season—called *The Jackie Robinson Story*. I struggled with how we as a white race could be so cruel to other human beings just because of the color of their skin. The indignities that he was forced to suffer make me cringe to this day. I don't know many guys who could have handled the insults and venom directed Jackie's way. I wonder how white players in his day would have reacted if the roles had been reversed.

Jackie Robinson was born in Georgia in 1919, the fifth child of a sharecropper, the grandson of a slave. His father abandoned the family and left with another woman when Jackie was two months old; he never saw or heard from his father again, so there was no male role model in the home. His mother moved the family to Pasadena, a Los Angeles suburb. Jackie seemed to have a chip on his shoulder growing up—not that I blame him much since he grew up in a racist society with the cards dealt against him. He was one heck of an athlete, though, and as you'll see, baseball may not have been his best sport.

Following high school graduation, Jackie attended Pasadena Junior College for two years and UCLA for two years from 1937–40. He earned letters all four years in four sports: football, basketball, track, and baseball. Some observers believe he may have been one of the best all-around athletes of all time. He was blessed with phenomenal hand-eye coordination: in 1936, he won the junior boys' singles championship in the annual Pacific Coast Negro Tennis Tournament; and later, he captured the table-tennis championship of the Army while he was in the service.

Baseball coaches at Pasadena JC and UCLA had to share Jackie with the track team. He'd often compete in the broad jump (before it became known as the long jump) in the morning and jump in the car and change into his uniform as his driver sped him to a baseball game. With little practice, Robinson won the NCAA title and would have been an Olympic medal favorite if World War II hadn't canceled the Olympic Games in 1940.

Jackie was quite a runner on the gridiron. His "catch-me-if-you-can" running style had defenders grasping at air as he swivel-hipped his way down the field. He also passed for seven touchdowns, kicked three field goals, and intercepted passes (most players went both ways in those days). At UCLA, he *averaged* twelve yards per carry and was named to various All-American teams.

As soon as the football players put away their pads, Jackie donned sneakers and played basketball. While at UCLA, he led the southern division of the Pacific Coast Conference in scoring and even played some pro ball in 1947.

Baseball is what we know Jackie Robinson for, and he starred at Pasadena JC and UCLA. But he also played on other teams, including the Pasadena Sox, a group of players from the Pasadena recreation department baseball school. In March 1938, Jackie, then nineteen and the team's shortstop, played an exhibition game against the Chicago White Sox, who conducted spring training in Pasadena. Jackie got two of the team's six hits against live major league pitching and impressed the White Sox coaches with his play. Manager Jimmy Dykes told reporters after the game, "If that Robinson kid was white, I'd sign him right now. No one in the American League can make plays like that."

Ah, but Jackie wasn't white, and he smoldered. Some of that edge was taken off when he began listening to a black minister named Karl Down while he was still at UCLA. He began seeing that God had a purpose for his life. He was drafted into the army after Pearl Harbor and after completing basic training, he was shipped off to Fort Hood for Officer Candidate School. One day, he boarded a military bus and took a seat in the front half of the bus. In the Jim Crow South, blacks had to give way and move to the back of the bus to make room for whites, but not in the military at that time. New regulations called for desegregation of military buses.

Jackie was not the cringing, humble-servant type, so he didn't exactly get up out of his seat when a white officer told him to go to the back of the bus. Like Rosa Parks would do twelve years later, Jackie refused to budge.

For this act of defiance, Jackie was court-martialed on a charge of insubordination, but fortunately for him, a tribunal exonerated him. The military was finished with him, however, and Jackie was given an honorable discharge.

Jackie came out of the Army needing to earn some money. He had worked out with the Chicago White Sox during their 1942 spring training in Pasadena and impressed manager Jimmy Dykes again. "He's worth $50,000 of any owner's money," he said, but the White Sox never made an offer.

He played semipro football, but the better money was in the Negro Leagues. Jackie joined the Kansas City Monarchs in 1945 and quickly made a huge impression on the Brooklyn Dodger scouts employed by Branch Rickey. As the Mahatma narrowed down his choice of who would be the first black person he would sign, he believed that Jackie's apparent strength of character would help him withstand the pressures that would undoubtedly ensue.

One of the ironies about the Jackie Robinson story is that he, too, was a Methodist, just like Branch Rickey. John Wesley, who founded the Methodist movement, called for social justice inspired and informed by piety to God. (Few people know this, but Branch Rickey's full name is Wesley Branch Rickey.)

So imagine the scene. It's August 28, 1945, and Branch Rickey has invited Jackie into his office to discuss a contract. Jackie assumed that he would be receiving an offer to play for the all-black Brown Dodgers team that Mr. Rickey was putting together for the Negro Leagues. Mr. Rickey lit a cigar and took his time before saying, "I brought you here to play for the Brooklyn Dodgers—if you can!"

That made Jackie sit up in his chair. Then Mr. Rickey, for three grueling hours, proceeded to role-play a succession of racists and bigots that he would surely run into. He role-played an insulting fan, a mean-spirited player, a snobby hotel manager, a rude headwaiter, a vitriolic sportswriter, and a vicious teammate. He told the infielder that other players would come at him with spikes up on double-play balls, throw at his head, or get called out on strikes by racist umps.

"But Mr. Rickey, are you looking for a Negro who is afraid to fight back?" asked Jackie.

"Robinson, I'm looking for a ballplayer with guts enough *not* to fight back! You will symbolize a crucial cause. One incident, just one incident, can set it back twenty years."

The Brooklyn general manager then reached for a book called *The Life of Christ,* written by an Italian priest named Giovanni Papini. He read a section of the book dealing with Christ's saying to turn the other cheek when someone strikes you, quoting this Scripture: "Ye have heard that it hath been said, an eye for an eye, and a tooth for a tooth. But I say unto you, that ye resist not evil: but whosoever shall smite thee on thy right cheek, turn to him the other also."

Papini expounded on this by writing: "To answer blows with blows, evil deeds with evil deeds, is to meet the attacker on his ground. Only he who has conquered himself can conquer his enemies."

Mr. Rickey dramatically closed the book and faced Jackie. "Can you do it?" he asked. "I know that you are naturally combative, but will you promise that for the first three years in baseball, you will turn the other cheek? Three years—can you do it?"

"Mr. Rickey, I've got two cheeks. If you want to take this gamble, I'll promise you there will be no incidents." From the beginning, Jackie understood the impact he would make. "You may start with me, Mr. Rickey," he said at their historic meeting, "but you won't finish with me."

Jackson Lears, writing in the *New Republic* magazine, said that by quoting Scripture, Mr. Rickey "was hitting Robinson in the heart, invoking the Methodist Christianity that they shared."

I don't have room to catalog the terrible abuse that Jackie suffered, especially during that first season when he was the only black player in the major leagues. The comments ranged from incredibly stupid to incredibly invective. Frank J. Shaughnessy, president of the International League, said he was happy that Jackie got called up. "He is a great boy and deserves the chance. I feel certain he will make good. He was the best player in our league last year."

Great boy. Jackie was twenty-eight years old during his rookie year.

Then there were other incidents, like that one that happened during his first road series against the Philadelphia Phillies. Harold Parrott, the Dodger traveling secretary, said he had never heard racial venom and dugout filth like what some of the Phillie players sprayed on Jackie during that series. Ben Chapman, the Southern-born and Southern-bred manager, railed on Jackie's thick lips and the supposedly extra-thick Negro skull, which he said restricted brain growth to almost animal level when compared with white people. He yelled out to Jackie to go back where he belonged—picking cotton or swabbing out latrines. "You can't play, you black bum!" he screamed for everyone to hear. "You're only up here to draw those nigger bucks at the gate for Rickey!"

Can you believe this stuff they were hurling at him?

We will be forever indebted to Jackie Robinson for what he did and what he endured. Our country is better off for what he did. There's no doubt that his Christianity sustained him, and for that, he has my gratitude.

They Said It

> *"I had to fight hard against loneliness, abuse, and the knowledge that any mistake I made would be magnified because I was the only black man out there."*

—Jackie Robinson

> *"The way I figured it, I was even with baseball and baseball with me. The game had done much for me, and I had done much for it."*

—Jackie Robinson

WHERE HAVE YOU GONE, JOE DIMAGGIO?

49

I was just twelve years old when Simon & Garfunkel released "Mrs. Robinson," the title song from the movie *The Graduate*. It's one of the more famous songs from the 1960s, and it's probably best known for the following lyrics:

Where have you gone, Joe DiMaggio?
A nation turns its lonely eyes to you (Ooo ooo ooo)

What's that you say, Mrs. Robinson?
Joltin' Joe has left and gone away.

I was too young to understand the social importance of "Mrs. Robinson," but today I can see what songwriter Paul Simon was trying to say about those turbulent times—that a troubled society missed the hardworking ethos exemplified by the Yankee Clipper himself, Joe DiMaggio. The song was a lament to lost heroes and the inability of a culture to look up to anyone.

Paul Simon remembers walking into an Italian restaurant in Central Park South in 1968, just after "Mrs. Robinson" was released. Joe DiMaggio, the pride of the Yankees, was seated in the restaurant, so Simon walked over and introduced himself.

"Mr. DiMaggio, I'm Paul Simon. I'm the guy who wrote 'Mrs. Robinson,'" he said. DiMaggio invited him to sit for a moment.

"What does that mean—'Where have you gone . . . ?'" DiMaggio asked, adding that he was still doing ads for Mr. Coffee and a savings and loan bank, and that he had never gone anywhere. In fact, in Joe's mind, he was as popular as ever.

"The song is about heroes, a certain type of hero," Simon explained. "I'm not making fun of you."

Joe DiMaggio wasn't too sure, but if I were him, I would be honored to be held up in contrast to what was wrong with America during the tumultuous Sixties, a time of social upheaval that this country had never experienced and hasn't experienced since then.

Joe was miffed, however, and he thought about suing Simon & Garfunkel. He also thought he should have been paid for the use of his name.

That pretty much sums up who Joe DiMaggio was for the nearly fifty years he lived *after* he played his final season of baseball with the New York Yankees in 1951. In today's language of business, he was a "brand," someone who symbolized class, and that was the image he wanted portrayed by the media. He expected to be treated royally everywhere he went, just as he expected to be introduced as "Baseball's Greatest Living Player" whenever he appeared in public. If he ate in your restaurant, he expected the meal to be free. If he attended your sporting event, he expected the best seats in the house—comp. If he picked out a new car at your dealership, he expected you to let him drive it for free until he returned and picked out a new car. If he used your bank for safety deposit boxes and banking services, he never expected to be charged.

That's because he was Joe DiMaggio—and you weren't. That's why he usually showed up at celebrity golf tournaments without golf clubs, forcing sponsors to purchase a new set of clubs and a golf bag, which he took home.

That's the feeling I got after reading Richard Ben Cramer's controversial but exhaustive biography, *Joe DiMaggio: The Hero's Life*. The other feeling that struck me is this: How come the money got to be so important for Joe? Everything he did in the last thirty years of his life was about accumulating as much cash as he could. He stuffed so many hundred dollar bills into a safety deposit box in a savings and loan bank near the San Francisco airport that the bank manager told him, "Joe, don't put any more in there. We'll have to get it out with dynamite."

Remember my story about attending the big earthquake that hit just before Game 3 of the 1989 World Series? Well, Joe DiMaggio was at Candlestick that day, taking his seat in one of those special boxes installed for the Series on the field. According to Cramer, Joe was in just as much a hurry to get out of the stadium as Jan and I were. DiMaggio wasn't rushing to his home in the Marina district to check up on his sister, however. Instead, he was worried about the $600,000 in cash inside the house.

When Joe arrived in the Marina district, fire trucks were blocking streets, houses were ablaze, and no one was allowed to go back to their homes. Except for Joe DiMaggio. Firemen escorted him to his home and gave him time to grab some things. When he exited his home a few minutes later, he was hefting a large garbage bag by the neck. The bag was filled with cash that he had earned from signing shows—money, I would imagine, that he wanted to shield from IRS scrutiny.

Joe made tens of millions of dollars in the last twenty years of his life (he died at the age of eighty-four in 1999) signing memorabilia. As long as there was cash on the table, he was glad to sign. Cramer recounts a story about how DiMaggio's lawyer and confidant, Morris Engelberg, had Joe signing right up until the end of his life. Engelberg brought one hundred baseballs into the hospital room, and the dying DiMaggio scrawled his signature on ninety of them. I kid you not: Engelberg confirms that this happened in his book, *DiMaggio: Setting the Record Straight,* released in 2003.

I wonder what drove Joe at the end. The Gospel of Matthew quotes Jesus as saying, "Do not store up for yourselves treasures on earth, where moth and rust destroy, and where thieves break in and steal. But store up for yourselves treasures in heaven, where moth and rust do not destroy, and where thieves do not break in and steal. For where your treasure is, there your heart will be also" (Matthew 6:19–21).

So, what did Joe leave behind?

Joe left behind tens of thousands, maybe hundreds of thousands, of bats, balls, gloves, photos, and other memorabilia signed with his name. They are worth nothing to him now. He left behind an embittered and neglected wife (Dorothy Arnold), a second wife who committed suicide (Marilyn Monroe), and a forgotten and estranged son, Joe DiMaggio Jr., who became a homeless junkie in his later years. When Junior received his small inheritance (just $20,000 a year) a few months after his famous father's death, he bought a bunch of drugs and died from a crack overdose.

That got me thinking: What will I leave behind?

Will I leave behind a wife and two children who loved me? Will Tiffany and Jonathan take my Christian legacy to the next generation? Will I leave behind the values that I tried to live my life by?

Will I be remembered for making investments in others and being a good listener?

I hope so, because when death arrives with the finality of the last out, I'll be looking for a postgame handshake from Jesus Christ. I hope he's going to say:

"Well done, my good and faithful ballplayer."

SUBJECT INDEX

NAME INDEX